Born in Yorkshire in 1937, Tony Harrison is a poet and leading adapter and translator of classic drama, including *The Mysteries*, *The Oresteia* and *Phaedra Britannica* at the National Theatre. He was President the Classical Association in 1987–88.

by the same author

THE MYSTERIES

THE TRACKERS OF OXYRHYNCHUS

TONY HARRISON

faber and faber
LONDON · BOSTON

First published in 1990
by Faber and Faber Limited
3 Queen Square London WC1N 3AU
This new edition published in 1991

Printed in England by Clays Ltd, St Ives Plc

Tony Harrison is hereby identified as author of this work in accordance with
Section 77 of the Copyright, Designs and Patents Act 1988.

All rights whatsoever in this play are strictly reserved and all applications to
perform it or any of it must be made in advance, before rehearsals begin, to
Fraser and Dunlop (Scripts), The Chambers, Chelsea Harbour, London SW10.

A CIP record for this book is available from the British Library

ISBN 0-571-16306-8

CONTENTS

NOTE TO NEW EDITION

After the Delphi production, *The Trackers of Oxyrhynchus* was subsequently revived at the National Theatre, and the revised text performed there now appears on page 73. This production was also subsequently seen at Salt's Mill, Saltaire, Yorkshire and at Art Carnuntum near Vienna. As this second edition went to press a world tour was being planned for 1991 after further performances at the National Theatre.

INTRODUCTION

One

Something prepared me for Greek drama long before I knew a
word of ancient Greek, or had ever heard the names of Hecuba
or Oedipus. It began with the creation of what I call my
'orchestra' in the sense I later learned for that Greek word
meaning 'circular dancing place'. This 'orchestra' became my
first brooding ground and, I think, the first intimation of what
for me is the basic struggle of art. I was eight. We were
celebrating what was called VJ (Victory over Japan) night with
a large bonfire in the back street outside our house. The
atmosphere was more celebratory than I can ever remember
before or since, with normally taciturn people laughing,
singing, dancing at the end of a terrible war. Furniture was
brought out of houses to keep the blaze going. The fire became
so high the telephone wires were burned down. The paint on
our back gate blistered and peeled off. It went on all night and
in the morning I helped to douse the fire and shovel the ashes
into tea chests to be taken away. When the space was cleared
the celebratory bonfire had left a black circle of scorched
cobbles with thick scars of tar.

Forty-five years later the circle is still there. Looking into that
circle I once thought of it as the nightsky globe totally devoid of
stars, an annihilated universe. It was something like Byron's
vision in 'Darkness':

> I had a dream, which was not all a dream,
> The bright sun was extinguished, and the stars
> Did wander darkling in the eternal space . . .

It looked like this when my imagination couldn't cope with the
twentieth century. It was in this starless shape, even before I
became a poet, that I learned to relate our celebratory fire, with
the white-hot coils from domestic sofas, to that terrible form of
fire that brought about the 'VJ' when unleashed on Hiroshima
and Nagasaki in August 1945. One element for celebration and
terror. One space for the celebrant and the sufferer.

I began to learn to people that scorched orchestra only after an immersion in the drama of the ancient Greeks. Things just as 'dark' occurred in this orchestra of Dionysus but it was lit by the sun and was surrounded by a community as bonded in their watching as we had been by our celebratory blaze. It was a drama open-eyed about suffering but with a heart still open to celebration and physical affirmation. In the late twentieth century, what clues to existential survival could be found in an ancient drama which managed to face up to the worst things it could imagine and yet not banish the celebratory? What style permitted the sufferer and the celebrant to share the same space? What were the ways and means?

Though the texts of ancient drama are constantly annotated and re-annotated, some of the factors I have found essential to the drama's affirmation are often overlooked.

The first thing to observe about Greek drama is that it was staged in the common light of day. A shared space and a shared light. Our word 'theatre' is derived from the Greek word θεατρον, a place of seeing. Not only did the audience (οι θεχτες: 'those who see' in Greek) *see* the action of tragedy, not only did the audience *see* the actors and chorus but the actors and chorus *saw* the audience. They were all equally illuminated by the light of the sun. The lighting grid was the great globe itself. In Athens of the fifth century BC that 'obvious reciprocity', that Harbage found between actors and audience in Shakespeare's theatre, was created from the beginning of the experience by the shared space and shared light. When Bertolt Brecht writes in one of his theatre poems, *The Lighting*

Give us some light on the stage, electrician. How can we
Playwrights and actors put forward
Our images of the world in half darkness? The dim twilight
Induces sleep. But we need the audience's
Wakeful-, even watchful-ness. Let them
Do their dreaming in the light.

and when Yeats writes that in the theatre 'the essential thing is always full or almost full light because the actor comes first', and how he would like to compel a theatrical producer to 'produce some Shakespearian play with all the stage lights in every scene', applying that principle even to the storm scene in *King Lear*; when Peter Brook brought the houselights up at the end of the first act of *King Lear*, before the blinding of Gloucester; when Poel looked for a lighting which 'evoked the open air'; and when Granville Barker's plans for an 'exemplary theatre' included 'provisions for performing in daylight', a suggestion his biographer calls 'wonderfully radical', when all these men of the theatre made these statements and gestures, they were expressing, in their various ways, a deep nostalgia for the theatre of daylight.

The Greeks had no need of a lighting system to 'evoke the open air'. They had such a system in the sun, which linked audience and performers in a common light. There was no atmospheric darkening of the stage for illusionary effect, nor to conceal such a spectacle as the Oedipus with gouged eye-sockets. Voltaire's suggestion in his note to Corneille's preface to *Oedipe*, that dim lighting might make that terrible image tolerable, would make no sense to Sophocles, who has the blinded king described as a 'spectacle', something to be looked at, a θεαμα, from the same root of the verb 'to see', that gives us theatre. It is also as a 'spectacle', in the same Greek word, that Prometheus draws attention to himself and the injustice he suffers at the hands of Zeus. His final cry is to the 'common light' that unites actor and audience, theatrical space and outside world, the imaginary and the real.

This 'light common to all' (παντων κοινον φαος, *Prometheus Bound* 1091–2) is the first essential of ancient drama. The light is the first thing to be addressed by Prometheus or Alcestis or Ion and it is not only the illumination in the sense of the lighting that unites audience and performer in a shared experience but also in the sense of spiritual understanding. Things are brought, as Oedipus says 'εις το φως', to the light, or as we might say, 'to the light of day'. Shared space and shared light. How different from the darkened auditoria of our day.

A Greek theatrical mask is part of the existential survival gear. It gives the bearing of survival to the actor wearing it. It represents a commitment to seeing everything through the eyes that never close. It represents a commitment to going on speaking when the always open eyes have witnessed something unspeakable. The masks must witness the unendurable. That is why they are created with their eyes open. The mouth must continue to speak in situations where the human being would be speechless or screaming and unable to articulate its agony. The shared space and light allow this seeing and this speaking. The shared light begs a common language. The mask is always 'presented'. It sees the audience looking at it. It seems to see more people than a human eye. A chorus of masks patrols the attention of the audience. If you know you are seen you know you are being addressed, and you attend.

The space and light and the mask are created for a communal act of attention, a deep concentration in which the spellbinding metrical language also plays a primary part. Performability is not something injected afterwards into a text. Greek texts are created with the performability for that known space in the conditions of shared light, and created to be spoken in masks to an audience that is *seen* and never cut off in darkened seats. Above all, since the expression 'to see the light' in Greek means to live, the final sense is that of shared *life*. And it is to that life that the masked upright figure of Hecuba commits herself and us at the very end of *The Trojan Women* of Euripides, and not to the 'total nihilism' that Sartre found in the play.

But even that commitment to life was not the end of the drama. The broken Trojan refugees were not the final image. After every third play in a group of three tragedies, as *The Trojan Women* was, would come a satyr play written by the same author, with a chorus of what we can see as men in their animal condition, represented as half or three quarters man with horse or goat attributes and an erect phallus. The unease that is felt and has long been felt at the idea of the bloated celebrant following hard on the heels of the sufferer has been responsible, along with natural oblivion, for the loss of these plays, which amount to a quarter of the whole large output of the great dramatists, Aeschylus, Sophocles and Euripides.

With the loss of these plays we are lacking important clues to the wholeness of the Greek imagination, and its ability to absorb and yet not be defeated by the tragic. In the satyr play, that spirit of celebration, held in the dark solution of tragedy, is precipitated into release, and a release into the worship of the Dionysus who presided over the whole dramatic festival. In the one complete surviving satyr play, the *Cyclops* of Euripides, the very last line allows the chorus the prospect of being liberated finally from the dark shadow of the Cyclops Polyphemus and spend the rest of the time in the service of Bacchus. This journey back into the service of the presiding god seems to be paralleled by the release of the spirit back to the life of the senses at the end of the tragic journey. It is unlikely that the quaffing promised to the Dionysian band was one in which a drop was taken from the cup for the sufferers of the preceding tragedy, as at Passover one drop of wine is removed from the cup of joy for each of the ten plagues which befell Egypt at the time of the exodus, but the sensual relish for life and its affirmation must have been the spirit of the conclusion of the four plays. The satyrs are included in the wholeness of the tragic vision. They are not forgotten or forced out by pseudo 'refinement'.

Without the satyr play we cannot know enough about the way in which the Greek spirit coped with catastrophe. The residue of a few tragedies might give us the illusion of something resolutely high-minded but it is a distortion, with which post-Christian culture has been more comfortable than with the whole picture. The thought of tragedy and satyrs co-existing has not been easy even for the most comprehensive of scholars. Even Sir Arthur Pickard-Cambridge, to whom we are all indebted for the description of the material environment of Greek drama, has a problem characteristic of the scholarship on it:

> The problem which if baffling to modern and Christian readers – how it was possible for the same audience, possibly even on the same day, to be absorbed in the noblest tragedy

and pass immediately to the grossness, which . . . comedy
displayed for at least a century and a half – would not have
been appreciated by the Athenians of the fifth century, and it
is one which will never be completely solved.

The stress on Christian and *readers* helps us to understand the
problem. Christianity, with what D.H. Lawrence called 'its lust
for the end of the world', certainly drove a wedge into human
nature and subverted the wholeness of an earlier imagination.
The shrivelled private scope of readership rather than presence
in shared light and space made both parts of the Greek spirit
harder to accommodate. The essential catholicity of Greek
drama, the unity of tragedy and satyr play, has been betrayed
into divided and divisive categories, 'high' and 'low'. The
Byzantine compilers helped to initiate this process by choosing
only few representative tragedies for study. Discoveries outside
of this ancient selection include those plays that help to
undermine the view of drama as uniformly high-minded, even,
given its early period of history, straining for an acceptable
monotheistic maturity! The so-called 'alphabet' plays of
Euripides included not only the one surviving satyr play but also
the category-disturbing *Alcestis*, often termed 'proto-satyric'
because Euripides offered it in place of the satyr play as the
fourth play of his competition entry. In this play Euripides
introduced his 'satyr', in the shape of Herakles, into the very
body of the tragedy: the celebrant admitted before the tragic
section had come to an end. The playwright thus showed both
elements interwined, doing what Johnson said of Shakespeare,
depicting neither 'tragedy' nor 'comedy' but the real state of
'sublunary nature' in which '*at the same time* the reveler is
hasting to his wine and the mourner is burying his friend', or, in
the case of Herakles in *Alcestis*, getting drunk while Admetus is
burying his wife. It is, of course, precisely this quality in
Shakespeare that has given those who want their genius more
'refined' the same problems that classicists have had with Greek
drama. One such characteristic voice was that of Robert
Bridges, Poet Laureate from 1913 to 1930:

Shakespeare should not be put into the hands of the young without the warning that the foolish things in his plays were written to please the foolish, the filthy for the filthy, and the brutal for the brutal; and that if out of our veneration for his genius we are led to admire or even tolerate such things, we may be thereby not conforming ourselves to him, but only degrading ourselves to the level of his audience, and learning contamination from those wretched beings who can never be forgiven their share in preventing the greatest poet and dramatist of the world from being the best artist.

How far we already are from that shared space and light of the Greeks. The divided art is perpetuating divided audiences, divided societies. This audience of Shakespeare's time, so despised and patronized by the Poet Laureate, is exactly the same as that which Alfred Harbage thought should take some of the credit for the greatness of Shakespeare's plays. It was due in part to that 'obvious reciprocity' which also existed abundantly in ancient Athens. Harbage's account of the audience in Shakespeare's theatre immediately shows up all that is throughly undemocratic in the view of Bridges.

> Mere coincidence will not explain why every Elizabethan play addressed to a *sector* of the people, high or low, learned or unlearned, is inferior in quality; why neither university nor law school, nor guild hall, nor princely banquet house begat dramatic poetry comparable to what came from the public theatres; or why Blackfriars failed to sustain the level achieved by the Globe. The drama reached its peak when the audience formed *a great amalgam*, and it began its decline when the amalgam was split in two.

If we stress the 'free' and the 'men' of 'freemen of Athens' we have a similar 'great amalgam' in ancient Athens, despite the fact it seems highly likely that slaves and even women were not at the theatres. A recent survey has shown that modern theatre audiences are composed of élite and privileged *sectors* of our society. For two of the greatest moments in world drama it seems to have been otherwise. W.B. Stanford has shown that the Athenian audiences were not simply intellectuals and sophisticated citizens but 'farmers, craftsmen, shopkeepers, manual labourers in far greater numbers than the priests, poets, philosophers and sophists'. He tells us that we should do well to remember that when it came to voting for the groups of four plays submitted in the competition the vote of a shoemaker was as good as a vote from a philosopher. The social composition of the audience in that shared space and shared light was not only a 'great amalgam' but could see that it was. Those gathered together had that kind of recognition of each other as belonging to the same society, but would only gather together on these important festival occasions; the uniqueness of the event also united them. We might say that TV reaches such an amalgam, but it is not present in the same space: TV viewers are not aware of each other attending, and therefore sharing not only the space and the light, but the illumination in the spiritual sense. When drama lost those conditions it became less able to bear and digest the worst things it could imagine. Dramas became texts divided into 'high' and 'low' art. The loss of satyr plays is both a symptom and a consequence of this division. What is lost is a clue to the wholeness of the Greek imagination and its deep compulsion to unite sufferer and celebrant in the same space and light. In the end those who feel excluded from 'high' art and relegated to 'low' will sooner or later want to destroy what they are not allowed to inhabit.

If we have a nostalgia for the theatre of daylight it is a sign of regret for a culture where the celebrant is born out of tragedy before our eyes. With us the masque and the anti-masque are as divided, as they were when Shelley saw that division as both the 'sign and the thing signified' in his regrettably uncompleted drama *Charles I* of 1819:

> Ay, there they are –
> Nobles, and sons of nobles, patentees,
> Monopolists, and stewards of this poor farm,
> On whose lean sheep sit the prophetic crows,
> Here is the pomp that strips the houseless orphan,
> Here is the pride that breaks the desolate heart.

These are not the lilies glorious as Solomon,
Who toil not, neither do they spin, – unless
It be the webs they catch poor rogues withal.
Here is the surfeit which to them who earn
The niggard wages of the earth, scarce leaves
The tithe that will support them till they crawl
Back to her cold hard bosom. Here is health
Followed by grim disease, glory by shame,
Waste by lame famine, wealth by squalid want,
And England's sin by England's punishment.
And, as the effect pursues the cause foregone,
Lo, giving substance to my words, behold
At once the sign and the thing signified –
A troop of cripples, beggars, and lean outcasts,
Horsed upon stumbling jades, carted with dung,
Dragged for a day from cellars and low cabins
And rotten hiding-holes, to point the moral
Of this presentiment, and bring up the rear
Of painted pomp with misery!

THE YOUTH

'Tis but

The anti-masque, and serves as discords do
In sweeter music. Who would love May flowers
If they succeeded not to Winter's flaw;
Or day unchanged by night; or joy itself
Without the touch of sorrow?

SECOND CITIZEN

I and thou –

A MARSHALSMAN

Place, give place!

And the Marshalsmen of division go on crying 'place, give place' in all our palaces of culture still.

Two

In 1907 Grenfell & Hunt, the Holmes and Watson of Oxford papyrology, discovered the tattered remains of a lost satyr play of Sophocles, the *Ichneutae* ('The Trackers'). The discovery of the papyrus with some 400 incomplete lines was announced at the Annual General Meeting of the Egypt Exploration Society by Dr Hunt, in the following words:

. . . Three years ago we were indebted to Oxyrhynchus for some extensive remains of a lost tragedy of Euripides, the *Hypsipyle*. It is now the turn of Sophocles; and most fortunately the discovery to which I refer represents a side of the poet concerning which we have been very much in the dark. As you know, it was customary to produce tragedies in trilogies, or sets of three, which were followed by a Satyric drama, a lighter piece in which the chorus consisted of Satyrs, and the high tension of the preceding tragedies was relaxed. Only one specimen of such a Satyric drama has come down to us, the *Cyclops* of Euripides. Of the work of Sophocles, as of Aeschylus, in this line there exist only short disjointed fragments preserved in citations by grammarians and others. I am glad to say that for Sophocles what may be considered a fair sample is now recovered.

When found, the papyrus in question was, as usual, much broken up; in fact, the various fragments were not even all obtained in the same year. But they have fitted together remarkably well, and as now arranged make up the first sixteen columns of the play, accounting for over 400 lines, of which about one half are complete or easily completed, and many more sufficiently well preserved to be intelligible. Since the length of a Satyric drama seems to have been considerably less than that of the ordinary tragedy, the amount recovered may well represent as much as half of the original whole. The play is the *Ichneutae*, or 'The Trackers', of which practically nothing beyond the title was previously known. It is based upon the familiar myth of the exploits of the infant god Hermes – his theft of Apollo's cattle and his invention of the lyre. Apollo, in an opening speech, announces the loss of the cattle, for which he has vainly sought, and offers rewards to the finder. Silenus then appears with his attendant Satyrs, and proposes to join in the search.

Encouraged by Silenus, the chorus start out on the quest –
they are the 'Trackers' from whom the play is named. They
soon discover traces of the cattle, leading to the entrance of a
cave; but here they are alarmed by curious sounds which they
do not understand – the notes of the newly-invented lyre with
which Hermes is amusing himself down below. Silenus
upbraids them for their timidity, and at length himself
knocks at the barrier, and a nymph emerges. In answer to
their questions, she explains that she is the nurse of the child
who has been lately born to Zeus, and whose abnormal
growth is so startling, and tells them of his invention of the
lyre. But she stoutly defends him against the imputation of
being concerned in the theft. They remain unconvinced;
some cowhide admittedly has been used in making the lyre,
and there are tell-tale tracks on the ground. While the
dispute is in progress Apollo returns, and accepts the
evidence offered by Silenus and the Satyrs as entitling them
to the promised reward. Here the papyrus breaks off; no
doubt in the sequel Hermes appeared on the scene and
appeased Apollo by the gift of the lyre, as narrated in the
Homeric hymn.

The piece was thus slight enough. Like the *Cyclops* of
Euripides, it is a short and simple dramatisation of a well-
known story, to which a Satyric setting was appropriate. An
element of comedy was supplied by the grotesque figures of
Silenus and the chorus, whose imitation of dogs upon the
scent lends itself to some rather broad humour. While
bearing the unmistakable Sophoclean stamp, this play thus
differs entirely in theme and treatment from the other plays
of Sophocles which we possess; and it fills up to some extent
a gap in our knowledge of the dramatist's art.

Three

As Dr Hunt says, we can probably assume that in the gaps of
the papyrus Hermes appeared and appeased Apollo by the gift
of the lyre, and certainly in the Homeric *Hymn to Hermes* the

infant inventor makes a mollifying benefaction to the god. The story goes as follows in Shelley's version of the hymn:

LXXXII

'Thou canst seek out and compass all that wit
    Can find or teach; – yet since thou wilt, come take
The lyre – be mine the glory giving it –
    Strike the sweet chords, and sing aloud, and wake
The joyous pleasure out of many a fit
    Of tranced sound – and with fleet fingers make
Thy liquid-voiced comrade talk with thee, –
It can talk measured music eloquently.

LXXXII

'Then bear it boldly to the revel loud,
    Love-wakening dance, or feast of solemn state,
A joy by night or day – for those endowed
    With art and wisdom who interrogate
It teaches, babbling in delightful mood
    All things which make the spirit most elate,
Soothing the mind with sweet familiar play,
Chasing the heavy shadows of dismay.

LXXXIII

'To those who are unskilled in its sweet tongue,
    Though they should question most impetuously
Its hidden soul, it gossips something wrong –
    Some senseless and impertinent reply.
But thou who art as wise as thou art strong
    Canst compass all that thou desirest. I
Present thee with this music-flowing shell,
Knowing thou canst interrogate it well.

LXXXIV

'And let us two henceforth together feed
    On this green mountain slope and pastoral plain,
The herds in litigation – they will breed
    Quickly enough to recompense our pain,

If to the bulls and cows we take good heed; –
    And thou, though somewhat over fond of gain,
    Grudge me not half the profit.' Having spoke
    The shell he proffered, and Apollo took.

But there is an alternative version to this story of the tranquil
takeover of the lyre, just as there is an alternative version of the
story of the peaceful transition of the shrine of Delphi from
Gaia to Apollo as told, for example, in the *Oresteia*. In some
stories Apollo bludgeoned his way into possessing what was
once a female shrine 'And Apollo took'! In the Valley of the
Muses, near Askra, the birthplace of Hesiod, in Euboea, which
I visited in 1987, and again after the première of *The Trackers
of Oxyrhynchus*, there was once, according to Pausanias, who
saw it, a bronze of Apollo and Hermes *fighting* for the lyre.

In these thorn-strewn slopes leading up to the summit of
Helicon there were not only statues to the Muses, looted by
Constantine, and the one mentioned by Pausanias representing
the struggle of Apollo and Hermes for the lyre. There were also
other cautionary bronzes. There was a statue of Thamyris
shown blind, with his lyre shattered at his feet. He was blinded
for his presumption in offering competition on the lyre. Near by
was a statue of Linus, killed by Apollo for offering him rivalry
in singing. Pausanias doesn't mention that there was a bronze of
Marsyas, the satyr, flayed alive for competing on the flute
against Apollo's lyre. For the divine patron of music and
poetry, the Parnassian supremo, this is appalling savagery, but
this pugnacity and paranoid possessiveness are characteristic of
Apollo's early transition from macho cowpoke to cultural
impresario. Rival lyre players, singers, upstart satyr flautists,
flayed, butchered, blinded, were set up as deterrents in the
Valley of the Muses and elsewhere. Herodotus says that the
skin of Marsyas was pegged out in a public square in Celaenae
(in what is now Turkey) and though it vibrated sympathetically
to any Phrygian air, remained stubbornly silent when hymns in
praise of Apollo were played in its vicinity. We are told that
Apollo had the flute of Marsyas hung up as a trophy in his
temple at Sicyon in the Peloponnese. Apollo was only

reconciled to the flute he always abhorred after his competition with Marsyas, when it was used by the flute player Sakadas to play a hymn to the god in Delphi. Flute-players are admitted if they play the Paean to Apollo. It seems that the flute of Marsyas did not show the same loyalty to its first animator as the 'the auld Orange Flute' or indeed the skin flayed from the flautist himself.

The Roman emperors Augustus and Nero both loved to dress up as Apollo and it was probably the lyre of Apollo that Nero 'fiddled' on while Rome went up in flames, a cool behaviour long endorsed by Apollo himself. A few months ago in Nicosia I saw a sign saying 'Apollo: Quality Underwear' and I suppose the Y-front endorsement is appropriate, as the male ego has had aeons of Apollonian support. His contemporary endorsements include an answering machine and a particularly repellent form of torture used in the prisons of Iran. In some manifestations Apollo would not have shied away from the vast statue that Hitler had planned for him in Berlin. And yet, everywhere, his image is at the apex of the pediment of our palaces of art.

Four

It was in Delphi, so powerfully presided over by Apollo, that *The Trackers of Oxyrhynchus* had its unique one-performance world première on 12 July 1988 in the ancient stadium. It was a joint production between the National Theatre Studio and the European Cultural Centre of Delphi. I have always wanted to prepare a piece for *one* performance. This was what the ancient dramatists did. In the theatre I most admire, poets, and I stress poets, wrote for actors they knew and for a space they knew.

From the beginning, this text was created for two actors, both Yorkshiremen, who had worked with me before in *The Oresteia* and *The Mysteries*. I created the part of Grenfell/Apollo for Jack Shepherd and the part of Hunt/Silenus for Barrie Rutter. It is more than half the battle of creation to know the instruments you are writing for. The space, too, was important. The International Meeting of Ancient Drama which takes place in Delphi every year was inspired by the first festival at Delphi set up by the Greek poet Angelos Sikelianos and his American wife, Eva Palmer, in 1927. For their dramatic performances they used the ancient theatre, lower down the slope and closer to the Temple of Apollo. Nowadays the ancient stadium is used, but with a wooden platform at one end of the racetrack, as if that differently structured curve at one end were the seating of an ancient theatrical space. I resolved to dispense with the platform and use the entire stadium space. This helped to dramatize a contemporary division in our culture between sport and art. In the Pythian Games with its athletics and flute contests, poetry and drama, held on this site, such a division would have been incomprehensible. As would the division between tragedy and satyr play, 'high' art and 'low' art. And in honour of that ancient wholeness we performed our piece, and we became *Ichneutae*, 'Trackers', seeking in fragments of our past and present a common wholeness, a common illumination, a common commitment to survival.

Five

Our 'technical' rehearsals lasted throughout the night of the 11th until after dawn on the 12th. The night had had unusual wild weather and the rocks of the Phaedriades surrounding the stadium concentrated and confined the winds there. The expedition tent of Grenfell and Hunt was blown away. Our papyrus flapped and struggled to be free and fly off to join the eagles that hung over Delphi. We never finished our rehearsal. I had to cover the possibility that the same thing might happen on the 12th. The relay race I had planned, to define the space of the stadium and give us ghosts of its ancient function to awaken the roars of the thousands who once sat at the Pythian Games, had unfortunately dwindled down to one solitary runner who ran like an ancient Marathon runner bearing an Olympic, or should we say Pythian, torch.

Three hours before our première I wrote and gave the following lines to Barrie Rutter to cover both for the expectation of new destructive gusts and to accommodate the solitary, message-bearing runner:

> Everything we've searched for, everything we found
> goes in Grenfell's mania, round and round.
> Grenfell's recurrent nightmare recreates
> careering caravans of Oxyrhynchus crates,
> crates of papyri in a never ending train
> and fragments like a hurricane hurtling through his brain
> and voices, thousands, from the ancient past
> exhorting him to find the 'Ichneftes' FAST!
> That's Grenfell's nightmare and I could add
> another like it that could make everybody mad.
> That the play in the papyrus should reach the light
> in the Stadium of Delphi on a very windy night.
> Last night the wind blew and it stripped
> the stage of everything but actors and a script.
> Let's concentrate, and despite the gusty weather,
> reconstruct the 'Ichneftes' μαζι 'together'.
> Memory runs a marathon, a human mind relay
> from century to century to recreate our play.
> Memory, mother of the Muses, frees
> from oblivion the 'Ichneftes' of Sophocles.

T. H., Newcastle-upon-Tyne, 1989

THE DELPHI TEXT

CHARACTERS

BERNARD PYNE GRENFELL/APOLLO
ARTHUR SURRIDGE HUNT/SILENUS
KYLLENE
HERMES
CHORUS OF FELLAHEEN/SATYRS/FOOTBALL
HOOLIGANS

This play was first performed in the Ancient Stadium of Delphi, Greece, on 12 July 1988, with the following company:

GRENFELL/APOLLO	Jack Shepherd
HUNT/SILENUS	Barrie Rutter
KYLLENE	Juliet Stevenson
HERMES	Dave Hill
	Peter Andrew
CHORUS OF FELLAHEEN/SATYRS/	Christopher Beck
FOOTBALL HOOLIGANS	Stephen Bent
	Jim Bywater
	Lawrence Evans
	Billy Fellows
	Dave Hill
	John O'Hara
	Philip Middlemiss
	Stephen Petcher
	Simon Rackham
	Clive Rowe
Director	Tony Harrison
Design and Lighting	Jocelyn Herbert
Composer	Stephen Edwards
Music Director	Dave Osbon
Company Stage Manager	Trish Montemuro
Stage Manager	Chantal Hauser
Sound	John Rule
Assistant Lighting Designer	Paul McLeish
Scene Painters and Lighting Operators	Chris Bowlby
	Luke Hallam
	Jane Harrison
	Max Harrison
Dance Arranger	Lawrence Evans
Assistant to the Designer	Vicki Hallam
Design Apprentice	Tim Hatley

ACKNOWLEDGEMENTS

Grateful thanks for support and assistance in bringing
The Trackers of Oxyrhynchus to the Ancient Stadium of Delphi
are due to:
    The John S. Cohen Foundation
    The Leventis Foundation
    Dr Marianne McDonald
Oliver Taplin and François Lissarague were also most generous
with enthusiasm and inside knowledge of satyrdom.

Photographs pp. 5, 8 by Vicki Hallam, pp. 6, 7 by Sandra
Lousada, pp. 72, 74, 76 by Nobby Clark.

Rehearsals in the Ancient Stadium of Delphi with backdrops
of papyri and behind them the Phaedriades

Grenfell (Jack Shepherd) and Hunt (Barrie Rutter) sorting
papyri in front of the expedition tent

Kyllene (Juliet Stevenson)

Satyrs burst out of the Egypt Exploration Fund crates
(performance 12 July 1988)

The Satyrs cavort

Silenus (Barrie Rutter)

8

BERNARD PYNE GRENFELL *(1869–1926) and* ARTHUR
SURRIDGE HUNT *(1871–1934), the Holmes and Watson of
British papyrology, are in the typical gear of Englishmen in the
desert, baggy khaki shorts, solar topis. There is a tent and outside
it a table made from expedition crates at which* HUNT *sits,
logging the finds of the papyri rolls that* GRENFELL *hands him.
They are both supervising a* CHORUS OF FELLAHEEN *who
from a mound of sand are extracting rolls of papyrus which are
passed along the chain of twelve, thrown, juggled, until they
finally reach* GRENFELL *who scrutinizes them and rapidly
interprets their contents. There are smaller mounds of sand
between the main one and the expedition tent. They represent the
rubbish mounds of the ancient Egyptian town of Oxyrhynchus.
There are numerous expedition crates scattered around waiting to
be filled with accumulated papyri and eventually carted away on
simple, rough carts. The crates are marked 'Egypt Exploration
Fund'.*

As the CHORUS OF FELLAHEEN *scrabble for, extract,
produce, throw, and juggle the papyri, they make a chant formed
from the lost plays of Sophocles, with the refrain:* Ichneutae
(*Ιχνεуτές*) Ichneutae (*Ιχνεуτές*) Ichneutae (*Ιχνεуτές*).

GRENFELL

We're trackers (Ιχνευτες) and what we seek
are fragments of papyri in ancient Greek.
We've filled a few crates full already this week.
Here are treasures crated, waiting to be shipped
from Egypt back to Oxford where we work out each script.
First we dig, then we decipher, then we must
deduce all the letters that have mouldered into dust.

Here at Oxyrhynchus where there's never been much rain
are rubbish heaps of riches. All these mounds contain
preserved papyri from the distant past.
These mounds need excavating fast . . . fast . . . fast.

9

Rubbish heaps of riches! Quite a paradox
there are priceless papyri in every crate and box,
from mundane wage bills for labour on a road
to fragments of a long-lost Sapphic Ode.
These chaps, our fellaheen, can't see what's unique
about scraps of old papyrus in ancient Greek.
We ship back papyri to decipher them at Queen's
but they'd use them, if we let them, as compost for their gr
Bits of Sappho, Sophocles and Plato
used as compost for the carrot and potato!

Papyri! Insects gnaw them. Time corrodes
and native plants get potted in a mulch of Pindar's Odes!
Horrible to contemplate! How can a person sleep
while Sophocles is rotting on an ancient rubbish heap?
Our fellaheen, though, are not entirely sure
if Menander's not more use to them as manure!
They ferret for fertilizer, and Hunt and I track
for philosophy and drama in nitrogenous *sebakh*.
Spinach now flourishes from the pulped-up roll
that held still hidden secrets of Sappho's soul.

Flinders Petrie's finds were the inspiration
that put us on the track of this present excavation.
(A hundred years ago exactly. The date
was July 1888.)
Petrie dug Hawara, and discovered there
a papyrus of Homer with a lock of lady's hair.
A hundred years ago almost to the day
I gazed on that Homer in a Bodleian display.
I swore, while still a teenager at Queen's,
to rescue Greek papyri from enriching Egypt's greens.
I was restless, restless. I could scarcely ever rest.
I became, I suppose, quite utterly obsessed.
I lay awake thinking how one day I too might
bring forgotten masterworks back to the light.

The first thing that I did was get a job
with Petrie excavating Coptos and Gurob.
Then after a tedious bureaucratic battle
I excavated Kum-Aushim and Umam-el-Atl.
By December I was able to bring Hunt out here
and '95 began our joint papyri-ing career.

(HUNT *comes out of tent*)

Here at Oxyrhynchus our excavations
lived up to, and surpassed, all expectations.
Crate after crate shipped off, load after load
from laundry list and ledgerwork to tragedy and ode.

(FELLAHEEN *activity increases. Exit* GRENFELL *into tent.*)

HUNT

We have *both* become obsessive. So many loads per hour
or they end up as compost on some Cairo cauliflower.
If one of our backs were turned our fellaheen
would be sloshing Bacchylides on their aubergine.
If we're not double-quick the local folk
will mix Homer and camel dung to grow their artichoke.
Find any fragment however frail or teeny
before it goes to fertilize fellaheen *zucchini*.
I suppose that a compost of ancient Greeks
as good a way as any to grow successful leeks.
We had to be a bit manic not to slip behind,
one digging and deciphering, one logging each new find.

(GRENFELL *comes out of tent and goes back in.*)

Grenfell gets so anxious to recover even scraps
it's brought the poor chap almost close to a collapse.
Grenfell's fast at everything he does. He can *read*
what most people can't decipher at double speed.
Grenfell's electrical, so mercurial and quick
I often fear the work will make my old friend sick.

Grenfell's torrential, so dazzlingly fast
I sometimes fear his sanity might not last.
I worry about Grenfell. Only last year
he said the god Apollo was shouting in his ear.
Apollo pursuing him. Grenfell couldn't rest
till he became, I have to say, almost literally possessed.
He viewed the way our names were in conjuction –
Grenfell–Hunt as an Apollonian injunction.
He heard Apollo yammering for scraps and tatters
of some lost Sophoclean play called *The Tracking Satyrs*.
'Grenfell, Hunt!' he heard the voice abjure,
'Prevent Apollo's favourite play becoming mere manure.
Grenfell! Hunt!' The god's voice went on speaking
putting Grenfell in a panic of papyri-seeking.
Night and day the voice went. 'Grenfell, Bernard Pyne,
hunt for my papyrus. This order is divine!'

(FELLAHEEN *activity intensified. They extract, throw, juggle,
pass on the flying papyri, which* GRENFELL *opens, deciphers
and passes to the seated* HUNT *to log. Their chant goes under
and between the* GRENFELL/HUNT *exchanges.*)

GRENFELL
(*Deciphering papyri*)

> Petition concerning repayment of loan . . .
> Petition complaining of . . . moan . . . moan . . .
>   moan . . .

(*He passes papyrus impatiently to* HUNT *who logs and completes
the find.*)

HUNT
(*Half speed, writing down* GRENFELL*'s deciphering.*)

> Petition concerning repayment of loan
> Petition complaining of . . . non-payment of loan.

GRENFELL

Letter on beer tax to the ταραχευται 'mummifiers'.

HUNT

But ταραχευται might mean 'salt-fish suppliers'.

GRENFELL

It might! It might! It might! It might! It might!
God! I do wish some *literature* would come to light.

Petition, petition, receipt, receipt, receipt.
Orders for the payment of supplies of wheat.

HUNT

(*Half speed, writing*)

Petition, petition, receipt, receipt, receipt.
Orders for the payment of supplies of wheat.

GRENFELL

Petitions, petitions, receipts and leases . . .

HUNT

(*Half speed, writing*)

Petitions, petitions, receipts and leases . . .
Can't call these finds lost masterpieces.

KYLLENE

(*From inside tent*)

φοβος εχει με των τοτε κακων
η Δημνια χθων Υψιπυλην . . . woe, O woe

GRENFELL

Not now! Not now! We'll let you know!

(*To* HUNT)
Did you hear that, that tragic moan?

HUNT
Take a rest, Bernard. I can manage alone.

GRENFELL
(*Back to deciphering*)

Acknowledgement of loan of vegetable seed
and . . . and . . . and . . . the rest I can't read.

(*He hands papyrus to* HUNT.)

HUNT
(*Studies and completes.*)

Sale of donkey . . . 56 Drachs!

GRENFELL
Receipt for payment of cattle tax . . .

Petition, petition, Ptolemaic 2 AD . . .
and . . . and . . . and . . . now let me see! –
letter from Gemellius . . . (in terrible condition!)
Seems to be some sort of

(*He hands papyrus to* HUNT.)

HUNT
Petition!

GRENFELL
Fragments of accounts concerning wheat . . .
Arthur, the date . . . I admit defeat.

(*He hands papyrus to* HUNT.)

See if you can do better than me.

HUNT

2nd BC!

KYLLENE

(*From inside tent*)

ωs απολλυμαι κακως
οι φοβοι δ, εχουσι με, O woe! O woe!

GRENFELL

(*To* HUNT)

Did you hear that, like a woman's death-throes,
a cry from far away, so full of fear?

HUNT

(*Alarmed and concerned*)

I think you need rest. Go inside for a doze.
Don't want you laid up. I'll manage things here.
Don't want you laid up like you were last year.

GRENFELL

(*Ignoring* HUNT *and even more frantically passing on rolls*)

Census!

HUNT

Census!

GRENFELL

Petition, report, report, report.

HUNT

Petition, report, report, report.

15

GRENFELL

Judicial proceedings, minutes of the court.

HUNT

(*Half speed, writing*)

Judicial proceedings, minutes of the court.

GRENFELL

O, what's that! Something that I almost missed,
the verso of that Oxyrhynchus census list . . .

(*Pause to decipher.*)

O, it's . . . Pindar . . . Pindar . . . but not all there!
A paean for the people of . . . of . . . but where?
A paean by Pindar hitherto unknown . . .

(HUNT *rises from his table and they both scan the papyrus.*)

GRENFELL *and* HUNT

(*In almost childish wonder*)

A paean of Pindar hitherto unknown . . .

(*Reading the Greek together*)

Κασταλιας . . . . . Απολλωνος . . . . . θαμινα Δελφων!

A paean of Pindar hitherto unknown . . .
for the people of Delphi,
                                lost till this minute.

HUNT

Castalia

GRENFELL

(*Transfixed, listening for the god in his ear*)

16

Apollo!

Delphi! They're all in it!

(*The* CHORUS OF FELLAHEEN *switch from their 'searching chant' which has been present under the above and begin to chant to the audience in the stadium of Delphi Pindar's newly discovered 'Paean for the People of Delphi'.*)

Προς Ολυμπιου Διος σε, Χρυσεα
κλυτομαντι Πυθοι,
Λισσομαι Χαριτεσ –
σιν τε και συν Αφροδιτα,
εν ζαθεω με δεξαι χρονω
αοιδιμων Πιεριδων προφαταν.
υδατι γαρ επι Χαλκοπυλω
ψοφον αιων Κασταλιας
ορφανον ανδρων χορευσιος ηλθον
εταιs αμαχανιαν αλεξων
τεοισιν εμαιs τε τιμαις.
ητορι δε φιλω παιs ατε μητερι κεδνα
πειθομενος κατεβαν στεφανων
και θαλιαν τροφον αλσος Α –
πολλωνος τοθι, Λατοιδαν
θαμινα Δελφων κοραι χθονος ομφαλον
παρα σκιαεντα μελπομεναι
ποδι κροτεοντι γαν θοω.

(*The* CHORUS OF FELLAHEEN *complete their performance of the 'Paean for the People of Delphi', then fall to searching in the mounds of sand again. In the silence that follows we hear the* VOICE OF APOLLO *from the rear screen where his image from the Delphi plate is projected. The* VOICE OF APOLLO *is speaking the first fragmentary lines of the* Ichneutae *of Sophocles as if from the distant past.* GRENFELL, *who has been frozen in rapt attention since he discovered the word 'Apollo' in the Paean,*

17

and heard it chanted by the FELLAHEEN, *is being taken over
by* APOLLO. *He is partially on the way to 'becoming'* APOLLO.)

VOICE OF APOLLO

. . .]σ[. . .
. . . . . .]κιο[. . .
. . . . . .]πειτα[. . .
. . . .]πεσσυϑ[. . .
. . . . . .]γ[. . . . .]λ[. . .
. . . .]ω[. . .

(*then* GRENFELL *speaks to himself as* APOLLO *and begins a
frantic dialogue with his 'alter ego'.*)

GRENFELL
Apollo
That Paean was fine and full of my praises
but I want that play where I speak the phrases.

Grenfell
But I'm working as fast as I possibly can.
Apollo
I suppose that you are being only a man.
Grenfell
Please leave me alone. Please, please go away.
Apollo
I'll pursue you until you track down my play.
Grenfell
I promise. I promise. New get out of my mind.
Apollo
No, till you find it I'll stay right behind.
Grenfell
I have a pistol, Apollo. I might have to shoot.
Apollo
And you might just regret that, Grenfell, old fruit.
Find the papyrus and fill in the gaps!
Grenfell
I'm working too hard. I'm damned near to collapse.

18

Do you realize how much time we require?
Apollo
Do *you* realize I require my *lyre*?
Remember Cassandra. I brought her to heel.
Grenfell
I wouldn't have thought that I had her appeal.
Apollo
Don't be too sure! Just keep on the track
and remember Apollo's right at your back.
Somewhere there's a play where I come on first.
Grenfell
Stop it! Stop it! My brain's going to burst.
Such literary finds are exceedingly few
Apollo
Bernard, old boy, I'm counting on you.

Grenfell
(*Producing papyrus*)

I've found this one. Will this one do?
Apollo
If I get a part or a mention or two.
Grenfell
It's a poem praising Theon from 3 A D .
Apollo
Praising Theon! What about me?
Grenfell
Where may I ask did you study your Greek?
Apollo
What's dead to you, dear, I actually speak.
I know Greek a damn sight better than you.
επτατονον χειρεσσι . . . shall I construe?

(*Reads Greek rapidly:*)

επτατονον χειρεσσι λυρην πολυηχεα κρουων
την αυτος τα πρωτα καμες παρα ποσσι τεκουοης
'The lyre in exchange for the bulls of Apollo' . . .
The rest's difficult Greek that you might not follow.

19

Grenfell
Almost an alpha I think that you pass.
Apollo
You'll get gamma minus rammed up your arse.
But you know very well that this fragment won't do
There's not enough of it, I'm mute, and the you
isn't me that the poem's lines address
I want my play, my play, the *Ichneftés*
alas, long ago vanished into nothingness.

(*Begins the fragments again.*)
απαντα χρηοτα . . .
Grenfell
Go to hell!
HUNT
(*Looking up from his engrossing logging*)

Bernard, are you all right? Are you feeling unwell?

GRENFELL
I'm fine! I'm fine! I'm fine! I'm fine! I'm fine!
Apollo
(*Mimicking*)

Bernard! You'd better discover that play of mine.

(APOLLO *now taunts* GRENFELL *with more fragments of the lost play.*)

]αξ[. . . . . .]λιθι[. . . . . .]στρ[. . . . . .]μηπ[. . .
Grenfell
Leave me alone. You must let me sleep.
Apollo
. . .]αρου[. . . . . .]ουα[. . . . . .]ρια[. . .
Grenfell
Go away! Leave me! Get away from here.
Apollo
. . .]λει[. . . . . .]γ[. . . . . .]φλεβο[. . . . . .]μη[

20

Grenfell

Lost. Lost. In the limbo of history.

Apollo

. . .]ατημε[. . . . .]ονιου β[. . . . . .]μη φυ[. . .

Grenfell

I'm doing the utmost a mere mortal can do.

Apollo

απαντα χρηστα και . . . . . . something . . . . . . λειν

Grenfell

Stop it! I can't get that phrase from my brain.

Apollo

απαντα χρηστα και . . . . . . something . . . . . . λειν

Grenfell

Stop it! Stop it! You'll drive me insane.

Apollo

απαντα χρηστα και . . . . . . something . . . . . . λειν

Grenfell

I beg of you, *please*. Don't say that again.

Apollo

(*Changing the taunting fragment momentarily*)

. . .]σ[. . .] κιο [. . . . . .] πειτα [. . .]πεσσυθ[. . .
]γ[. . .]λ[. . . . . .]ω[. . .

What goes in the gaps, Grenfell? Come on, you know.

Grenfell

I don't! I don't. Go! Go! Go!

Apollo

απαντα χρηστα και . . . . . . something . . . λειν

You've got to use that mercurial brain
and put all my missing letters in,
from this instant I'm in you and using your skin.
Find me the play where these fragments go

. . .]σ[. . .]κιο[. . . . . .]πειτα[. . . . . .]πεσσυθ[
. . .]γ[. . .]λ[. . . . . .]ω[. . . *etc. etc.*

(*This fragment is now again in the air from the rear screen and*
GRENFELL *rushes round the expedition tent 'pursued' by*
APOLLO.

21

Finally, in panic and exasperation he fires his pistol at the imagined phantom of APOLLO. *This shot sets off a relay race between the* FELLAHEEN *in three teams of four, with papyrus rolls as batons. The 'relay race' (which also represents the race against time of Grenfell's and Hunt's papyrology) is run along the laid out tracks in the stadium from the front screen to the rear screen. We hear during the race, as the 'music', the sound of some 8000 ghosts 2000 years ago, say, in Pindar's time. The chants of these ancient spectators are based on fragments of the* Ichneutae. *These fragments we will, later, associate with the* CHORUS OF SATYRS. *The winning papyrus/baton is presented to* HUNT.)

VOICE OF APOLLO

. . .]σ[. . .
. . . . . .]κιο[. . .
. . . .]πειτα[. . .
. . . . . .]πεσσυϑ[. . .
. . . .]γ[. . .]λ[. . .]ω[. . .

(*Immediately we hear from the rear screen the 'Apollo' fragments which have the immediate effect of changing* GRENFELL *into* APOLLO, *or at least effecting the first stage of his transformation.* HUNT *goes into the expedition tent.*)

GRENFELL/APOLLO

(*Emerging from rubbish tip spitting out* APOLLO*'s fragments*)

. . .]σ[. . .
. . . . . .]κιο[. . .
. . . .]πειτα[. . .
. . . . . .]πεσσυϑ[. . .
. . . .]γ[. . .]λ[. . .]ω[. . .

I'm a god, Apollo, but I was tipped
on a rubbish heap inside this manuscript.
I've spent centuries asleep
on an Oxyrhynchus rubbish heap.

You can imagine my fine Olympian feelings
tossed on to a tip with old potato peelings.
Till 1907 I had to wait
when Grenfell and Hunt came to excavate.
Covered in rubbish! But what's much worse is
being resurrected with only half my verses.
Converted into dust and bookworm excreta,
riddled lines with just the ghost of their metre.
All my speeches, all my precious words
mounting mounds of dust and millipede turds.
Ages under rubbish, sand and desert heat
and then be resurrected only half complete.
One used to the heights of Mount Parnassos
buried under dirt and drab domestic dross.
That's bad enough. But fate's not really fair
to have me only half restored, and not all there!
It's pathetic! Half the things I say
time or the desert mites have gnawed away.

Enough complaining though. Now no more ado –
straight into the script and go right through.
And bit by bit we'll try to pick our way
slowly back through time and this lost satyr play.

Though I'm a deity and in everything divine
I still can get kerpertled about my kine.
You can't imagine how much it deeply grieves
even a god like me to lose his beeves.
My heart, though an immortal's, absolutely breaks
to think of all my loved ones turned into steaks.
It drives me out of my Apollonian mind
tracking down those cattle I just can't find.

Some light-fingered lout has filched my kine
that now could be kebabs washed down with wine.
Some villain, some unscrupulous thief's
probably turned my cows into ροσβιφ [*rosbif*]
I want them back at once or even sooner

23

before they're barbecued στα καρβομνα [*sta karvouna*]
Some dissembling cattle-rustling shit
's got them, at this minute, browning on his spit.
Even for a god the way's hard-going
ears pricked for the slightest sound of lowing.

(*Listens*)

Listen! Nothing! Listen! . . . Oh I knew
each of my darlings by her distinctive moo.

(*Calls Greek names*:)

Κανελλω μου . . . Ασπρουλα μου . . . Παρδαλω μου . . .
Λενιω μου . . . Αρχοντα μου . . . Μαρυουλα μου . . .
Αστηρης μου . . .

Listen! Nothing! Some despicable slob
has done a stealthy cattle-rustling job.
I've been all over Greece. So far. So far!
I bet my bulls are in some bugger's abattoir.
I've been so far, following their trail
the length and breadth of Greece to no avail.
Who'd commit the sacrilege? Who could steal
my little loved ones and convert them into veal?
For a moment I thought I could discern a
somewhat suspicious sniff from a taverna.
It seemed to me that smell might mean a
meal of my moo-cows swilled down with retsina.

I'm almost out of my godlike mind
tracking those nicked cows I just can't find.
Who'd commit the sacrilege? Who'd dare? Who'd dare
to spirit off my herd into the air?
Man or immortal? It's hard to believe
someone could have had the cheek to thieve
the cattle of the Sungod out of their byre.
I'm as furious as the Furies in the *Oresteia*.

24

Thessaly, Boeotia, the Doric (space . . . space . . .
space)
then quickly to Kyllene, that's this place.
So, shepherd, farmer, charcoal burner,
layabout in the taverna,
and, maybe in rustic parts like these,
descended from the dryades,
the children of wild woodland creatures
with half human and half goat/horse features,
if *any* find my cattle stolen from their lord,
Apollo, and returns them, he'll get a good reward.
There's bakhsheesh for the body who can track
down my stolen herd and bring them back.

HUNT

(*From inside tent*)

Grenfell, Bernard, are you sure you're all right?
Shall I come out and give you a hand?
Enough work for today. You'll ruin your sight.
It's too dark to decipher or dig in the sand.

APOLLO

Hunt!

HUNT

(*From inside tent*)

Just a minute, just getting dressed.

APOLLO

Hunt out more fragments and find me the rest.
Hunt!

HUNT

(*From inside tent*)

Coming!

25

APOLLO
Hunt for my kine.

(*From the expedition tent enter* HUNT *now as* PAPPA
SILENUS, *the leader of the* CHORUS OF SATYRS)

SILENUS
Ιασου, Apollo, care for some wine?

I heard your proclamation, sir, and ran
or came as quickly as an old geezer can.
Us satyrs can help you. Our horse-like sniffers
will soon track down your heisted bulls and heifers,
and, maybe, win, divine Apollo, Lord,
whatever you're offering by way of reward.
If you could see your way, your honour, to bestowing
bakhsheesh on the boys, I'll get them going.
Summat beneficial. They'd have no quarrel
with gold or food, or liquid from a barrel,
but don't reckon too much to a wreath of laurel.
Summat solid, Lord Apollo, please,
not leaf equivalents of OBEs.
A bit of wilting boskage for the brows
falls far short of casks for a carouse.
Or cash to buy the casks if the supply
of buckshee Dionysian has all run dry.
A nightmare too monstrous to take in
A thirst like mine and no wine in this skin –
The prospect of promotion to Sir Satyr
doesn't make my heart go pitter-patter.
You know us, all prancing, getting pissed
so forget your Olympian Honours List.
Summat solid. Are we both agreed?
If so, I'll get the lads out at top speed.

APOLLO
I must say I find you commendably keen.
I'll make you the foreman of my fellaheen.

26

I'll put you in charge of my trackers, I mean.

SILENUS

My boys'll do their bit. Your bulls'll get tracked
but the reward, remember. Don't forget our pact.
And now to the task in hand. Now, rightaway
I'll bring my loyal lads into the play.

(SILENUS *gazes towards the rear screen where the shadow
puppets of* SATYRS *are projected.* APOLLO *looks at them.*
APOLLO *stays gazing at the shadows which begin to move.*
SILENUS *turns towards the audience and takes out a referee's
whistle.*)

I'll whistle up those loyal lads of mine.

(SILENUS *blows the referee's whistle. The* SATYRS *move. But
do not enter. Blows again.* APOLLO *moves closer to rear screen.
Nothing.*)

APOLLO
(*Shouting back to* SILENUS)

You've lost your herd like me. I see no sign.

SILENUS

I assure you, sir, that's not the case. Oh no
my lads are like lightning just as I am slow.
All Pappa Silenus has to do is click
his fingers and they'll be here in just one tick.

(SILENUS *clicks his fingers.* APOLLO *stares. The shadows
move. But the* SATYRS *do not enter.*)

If I take my middle finger and my thumb
and click them together. They'll come. *They'll come!*

(SILENUS *clicks confidently.* APOLLO *stares at shadows. Nothing.*)

APOLLO
(*Moving even further up towards rear screen*)

Well? Well? Where are they? Nothing to be seen.
They're unreliable like the fellaheen.

SILENUS
There's only one thing left to try
a few new-found fragments from the *Ichneutae*.

Sorry, Erasmian! What I'm saying is if we shout
some fragments of *Ichneftés* my satyrs will come out.

(SILENUS *takes a papyrus scroll and unrolls it to reveal some fragements of the Greek papyrus, in fact, the first words of the Chorus of Satyrs in their fragmentary, incomplete state. They should be legible to all. With this he begins to teach the audience to chant the fragments until there is a strong chant which is echoed by the ancient voices of the 8000 ghosts at the ancient Pythian Games.*)

ιϑ αγε δ [. . . . . .]
ποδα βα [. . . . . .]
απαπαπ [. . . . . .]
ω ω σε τοι [. . . . . .]

(*To* APOLLO *waiting for the Satyrs*)

Are they coming out? Are all my satyrs here?

APOLLO
No, they're stuck in the papyrus and don't want to
appear.

(SILENUS *once more gets the audience to chant the fragments and once more the shadows move and the chant from the living audience is taken up by the 8000 ghosts of the Pythian Games*.)

SILENUS

ιϑ αγε δ] . . . . . . [
ποδα βα] . . . . . . [
απαπαπ] . . . . . . [
ω ω σε τοι] . . . . . . [

Haven't they appeared, your great Apolloship?

APOLLO
Not the faintest sign of a satyr phallus tip!

SILENUS
Just one more chorus of ιϑ αγε δ . . .

APOLLO
It's hopeless, like trying to bring back the dead.
But, if you must, one more chorus. Go ahead.
If you have any luck once you've got your lads out
I'll be down in my temple. Give me a shout.

(*Exit* APOLLO *towards the Temple of Apollo.*)

SILENUS

ιϑ αγε δ] . . . . . . [
ποδα βα] . . . . . . [
απαπαπ] . . . . . . [
ω ω σε τοι] . . . . . . [

(*The chant is repeated by the audience and echoed by the 8000 ghosts of the ancient Pythian Games who are watching an athletic contest.* APOLLO *is almost up to the rear screen waiting for the shadow puppets to emerge from the screen.*

SILENUS *cuts off the audience's chant, and in the ensuing silence suddenly the twelve crates stencilled 'Egypt Exploration*

29

Fund' fall open together revealing in each a SATYR *and so
forming a* CHORUS OF TWELVE SATYRS. *The twelve crates
open forwards, backwards and sideways and create a
labyrinthine platform of crosses on which are painted the tracks
of Apollo's herd. This maze platform is where the* SATYRS
*perform their dance. They wear clogs. These 'hoofs' make them
the original 'hoofers'.*

They pick up the chant of Greek fragments that SILENUS,
*the audience and the 8000 ghosts of the Pythian Games had
summoned them up with.*)

(*To audience and ghosts*)

> Ευχαριστω, you living. Ευχαριστω, you dead,
> you've brought my boys back with your ιϑ αγε δ.

(*To* SATYRS)

> After two thousand years, lads, look, there's your text.
> It's up to you, to track what comes next.
> And once you've tracked down each missing Greek
>   word
> then sniff out the trail of Apollo's lost herd.

CHORUS OF SATYRS
Group B
ιϑ αγε δ . . . . . . (bracket . . . bracket . . .)
Group C
ποδα βα . . . . . . (bracket . . . bracket . . .)
Group A
απαπαπ . . . . . . (bracket . . . bracket . . .)
Group B
ω ω σε τοι . . . . . . (bracket . . . bracket . . .)

Where cows tread . . . (track it . . . track it . . .)

Group C

near or far . . . (track it . . . track it . . .)

Group A

seek cow-clap . . . (track it . . . track it . . .)

Group B

however wee . . . (track it . . . track it . . .)

επιϑι κλωπ . . . . . . (βραψκετ . . .)

Group C

υπονομα κ . . . . . . (bracket . . .)

Group A

Don't give up hope . . . (track it . . .)

Group B

We'll get them back . . . (track it . . .)

(*The* CHORUS OF TWELVE SATYRS *now begin to follow the marked maze-like tracks and become a parody of the Furies in the National Theatre* Oresteia, *sniffing for the blood of Orestes. At first their respective tracks avoid one another, but only just.*)

Group B

Sniff, sniff
sniff at the track
we've gotta get t' god's cattle back.

Group C

Sniff, sniff
sniff at the dung
t'devil who did this is gonna get 'ung.

Group A

Sniff, sniff
sniff every turd
t'droppings'll lead us t'god's 'erd.

Group B

Sniff, sniff
sniff left and right
sniff every tincture of cattle shite.

31

Sniff, sniff
sniff every clue
sniff every sort of numero two.

Group A

Sniff, sniff
sniff without stopping
sniff every turd, sniff every dropping.

Group B

Sniff, sniff
sniff t'shit on t'ground
t'cattle-rustler's gotta be found.

(*The* SATYRS' *maze/tracking dance continues and becomes
faster as though they are getting closer to their prey, then,
following their different tracks they end in collision. They fall
down, then they begin to look at the tracks closely.*)

1

If these are bull's tracks, their back legs go first.
These bulls have had their bums reversed.

2

These tracks of god's herd, if that's what we've found
Look they're all of 'em the wrong way round.

3

Hey, look here at this! It's stupid, daft.
Their backlegs are forrad, their front legs aft.

4

Blow me some bugger's done a switch.
Head or arsehole, which is which?

5

Eeh bah gum, and ecky thump

32

this un's face must be in its rump.

6

Some force has sent us out of our minds
Cows don't moo from their behinds.

(*The* SATYRS *begin to track again. They reprise their chant,
and again end up colliding.*

*Suddenly there is an eerie sound which stops them dead in their
tracks. (This eerie sound is the sound of the newly invented lyre,
the first stringed instrument.) The* SATYRS' *clogs start
chattering with fear on the crate platform.*)

1

That sound!

2

'orrible!

3

Frightening!

4

Scary!

5

Spooky!

ALL

(*To audience*)
It's the prototype of the bazouki!

6

Don't care what it is. I'm off back in
that papyrus! Stuff all this tracking!

You're pathetic. You're all made of jelly.
Every man-beast of you's a yeller belly.
You cowardly creeps, you dastardly dogs
you're not fit to buckle or bull up my clogs.
The buzz of a few lobelia-browsing bees
has you lot trembling at the knees.
Some shepherd's yell, some midget poodle's yap
and your clogs are all clarted with panicker's crap.
Unmanned, un*horsed* by some moggy's meak miaou
made into cowards by one moo from a cow.

And if that sound had the merest hint of moo
it might be the herd these tracks have led to.
Scared of your own shadow, no spunk, no spine
all talk and tupping, no true sons of mine.
Bragging and shagging, that's your style
but show you real action and you run a mile.
You say you'll stick by me, but come the crunch
you turn out such a yeller-bellied bunch.

But Silenus in his day, he never fled.
He faced all dangers with no shred of dread.
Silenus the Satyr, never short of spunk,
braved every battle, never did a bunk.
He was a warrior, valorous, not weak,
not thrown in a panic by a mere squawk or squeak.
When fierce battle raged I never quit –
there I was always in the thick of it.
A hero with honour from many a campaign,
an honour your cowardice will now stain.
Think of an old soldier having to see
his own battalion turn tail and flee.
The ones he brags about as his 'brave boys'
ready to desert the field because of a mere noise,
some squawk, some squeak, some tu-whit-tu-whoo.
A fieldmouse's fart's enough to scare you.
Fabled as I am for many a noble feat

it breaks this soldier's heart to see you in retreat.

You'd piss off if you heard a parrot sneeze.

CHORUS OF SATYRS

1

Come here then, you hero, and play Hercules.

2

Yer, come here yourself, if you have no fear.

3

If you are so brave, then come over here.

4

It's all right for you. You're not even near.

5

If you brave dangers then brave this one now.

6

Ay, then tell us we're only scared of some cow.

7

Ay, show us this famous courage of yours.

8

And see how your feel when the grim monster roars.

9

You'll find out we're terrified with good cause.

10

It's a sound like nothing on earth before.

11

It strikes terror in us right down to the core.

If you know no fear be the first on the track.

SILENUS

I am the hunter and you are the pack
and the hunter, when tracking, leads from the back.
But if an old soldier has to instil
courage in cowards, then instil I will.
I'll lead the rabble, if you so choose
and pump up your courage with hunter's halloos.
When a fierce commander stands at their head
even base cowards forget to feel dread.
When cowards are led by commanders like me
they see my example, stand fast, and don't flee.

(SILENUS *puffs out his chest, stands erect, and begins to march
with as much dignity as he can muster the platform 'maze'. At
certain specified points he executes a hard-clog shuffle intended
to make the* SATYRS *take courage, stand, and then be prepared
to confront the eerie noise.*

One by one they begin to support the 'bravery dance' of
SILENUS. *The dance reaches a crescendo, then is cut off by the
sound of the hidden newly invented lyre.* SILENUS *hears it.*)

I'll let you do the tracking. I'm getting too old.

(*To audience*)

But I'll be back later for my share of the gold.

(*Exit* SILENUS *to a seat in the audience. But the* SATYRS *are
now heartened and determined to find the source of the strange
noise never heard on earth before. They begin a clattering dance
to rouse the nymph* KYLLENE *who is reposing in the expedition
'tent/tiring house'. Each time they reach a crescendo they stop
and then turn towards the tent, but* KYLLENE, *so eager before,
now misses her cue. During this time some* SATYRS *drop from*

36

*the dance and begin to build 'The Theatre of Dionysos' in front
of the front papyrus screen. They build this rough theatre from
the 'Egypt Exploration Fund' crates; some open on their sides to
allow three* SATYRS *to crouch and appear as though they are
supporting the stage like the figures in the Theatre of Dionysos in
Athens. The dance to rouse the nymph* KYLLENE *becomes
more urgent and then slower as the* SATYRS *get weary until only
one is left to finally rouse her from the tent.* KYLLENE *finally
emerges from the tent. She is a Caryatid, like those supporting
the pediment of the Erectheum in Athens. In as dignified way as
possible she places a vast piece of pediment on her head and
walks slowly from the tent to the stage created by the crates,
mounts the steps and enters on the stage through a gap in the
papyrus screen. Spotlight on screen. Behind the screen*
KYLLENE *ascends the steps.*)

KYLLENE
ως απολλυμαι κακως . . . O woe! O woe!

(*Enter* KYLLENE *through papyrus curtain.*)

(*Looking down from stage*)

I have a feeling I'm in the wrong show!

(*She speaks only 'high' dated Victorian verse of the kind that
Greek tragedy used to be translated in. Three* SATYRS *grunt
under the weight of the* σκηνη *[scene].*)

CHORUS OF SATYRS
I
So calm of body, so serene of face,
drapery discreet, and every hair in place.

2
Them girls are straight but we're not straight
but bent and straining underneath the weight.

37

3

Though it's tons of marble that she holds
A caryatid still looks like a centrefold.

4

The Theatre of Dionysos. Have you seen
the poor satyrs there supporting the scene?

5

We're only half human so we can be shown
sweating and straining underneath the stone.

6

Caryatids carry as their name suggests
but no sweat ever trickled down their breasts.

7

Caryatids carry tons of carved stone
but never let out a grunt or a groan.

8

Horse's ears and tails, but we still have souls
and we're always shoved into supporting roles.

9

Caryatids can, but satyrs aren't allowed
to carry tons of marble and still look proud.

10

Caryatids carry the Erectheum high
but their armpits stay unstinking and dry.

(*The haughty* KYLLENE *who has spent these speeches moving her pediment-loaded head from speaker to speaker, now begins to speak and breaks her silence to address those who have disturbed her calm.*)

KYLLENE

Bestial creatures! Wherefore have you brought
to this secluded spot your uproar foul?
What novel sports are these? They are not they
wherewith of old you made your master glad,
who clad in his fawnskin and with thyrsus high
was wont to chant of yore the holy hymns
with, for escort, nymphs and youthful throngs?

SATYR I

(*Under the stage*)

She means Dionysos, pissed, sang us old songs.

KYLLENE

Now I know not what possesseth you
nor what crazed folly spinneth you awry . . .
I heard like hunters' halloos from deep within
a cry when keen trackers close upon their prey
and hap upon the beast deep in its lair.
And then such harsh words as theft and thief
assailed my ears and some god's proclamation.
Your fragments of furore reached me down there
and then an utter cacophony commenced.
I feared that you would do my person harm.

SATYR I

(*Joining in 'tragic' tone*)

Stay thine anger, nymph of the deep zone.
We are no bringers of disruptive strife.
Nay, all that we humbly wish is that you disclose
the meaning of that hidden sound we heard.

KYLLENE

That is a better way to learn what you desire

39

than by alarming here a poor defenceless nymph.
Quarrels are most distressing to my soul.
Now I implore proceed and make your plea.

SATYR I

Ruler of this region, Kyllene, Queen,
our purpose later will I you explain.
But this voice we heard, what is it, pray?
It frayed our nerves and set our teeth on edge.
Who is it that bringeth the gooselumps on our flesh?
What is it that raiseth the spine hairs on our back?

KYLLENE

I must advise you ere I do commence,
should you disclose what I to you disclose,
there will be severest suffering in store.

SATYR 2
(*Groaning under weight of stage*)

I wish she'd get to t'point. My back's that sore.

KYLLENE

These things are secret, guarded by the gods.
The heavenly ones keep Hera in the dark.

SATYR 3
(*Under stage*)

Zeus, again, I bet, and some new lascivious lark!

KYLLENE

Zeus hither hied where Maia doth abide
and all unbeknownst to Hera, hither hied
and made the fair one his clandestine bride.

SATYR I
(*Under stage*)

40

Zeus never could resist a bit on t'side.

In the cave the nymph brought forth a son
the which, because his mother Maia
doth languish in a fever nurse I in these arms.
But the babe doth burgeon greatly day by day.
'Tis a great wonder to me and a fright.
Born six days ago and yet hath boyhood reached.
He blossometh and shooteth up without a pause.
Such is the babe whose nurture I have here.
We conceal him for his mighty father's sake.

SATYR I

(*Under stage*)

I wish I could escape, that babe sounds queer.

SATYR 2

(*Under stage*)

Gerronwi'it! Mi back's about to break.

KYLLENE
As for the voice which caused you such affright
bursting forth from some unseen source of sound
it came from something turned the wrong way up.
The babe I nurse devised it in a day
from a dead creature, as a source of joy.
He plays his strange device both night and day.

SATYR 3

(*Under stage*)

I hope that's the end. Mi back's giving way.

SATYR 4
Ay, bugger the whatsit, and the miraculous boy

41

wanking about with the dead creature toy.

SATYR 5

Excuse me, but how can summat dead, like, sing?

SATYR 6

Ay, how come a voice came from a dead thing?

SATYR 7

Dead but vocal! A corpse that can carol.

SATYR 8

Seems somebody's snout's been into the barrel.

SATYR 9

It's a stiff and it warbles. How come?

SATYR 10

Ay, how come?

KYLLENE

Dead it has a voice. Alive it was dumb.

SATYR 11

Give us a clue. Is it bent, fat, short or what?

KYLLENE

'Tis spotted and shaped somewhat like a pot.

SATYR 12

A leopard, of course, or some sort of cat.

KYLLENE

No, sorry. It isn't at all like that.

SATYR 4

Not a crab, not a lobster, not a crustacean?

SATYR 5

Then it's gotta be the bug part of creation.

SATYR 6

A beetle? The Etna horned scarab, mayhap?

SATYR 1

(*Under stage*)

Solve her damned riddle and cut all the crap.

(KYLLENE *moves the vast pediment on her head slowly in answer to the last guess*.)

SATYR 7

Madam, what bit of it makes that horrible din?

SATYR 8

Does that horrible noise come from outside or in?

KYLLENE

From what you might call the creature's crust.

SATYR 2

(*Under stage*)

Solve the bloody riddle. My head's going to bust.

SATYR 9

If we may be so presumptuous as to inquire.

KYLLENE

(*After a long pause during which the pediment-weighted head moves from one side to the other*.)

The beast's called a tortoise. The invention's the lyre.

(KYLLENE *indicates the lyre with the baby projected on the front screen. The* SATYRS *listen as the lyre sounds again.*)

CHORUS OF SATYRS
1

It could be a goat
to judge from its note

All
BUT!

2

It could be a duck's
the guts that he plucks

All
BUT!

3

It could be a cat
A cat sounds like that

All
BUT!

4

Dog's gut or hound's
could be making these sounds

All
BUT!

I bet it's bullock gut.

Summat's been flayed
for this sweet serenade

5

It's not just the tortoise's hollow shell
there's some other creature in there as well.

44

All

Summat's been flayed
for this sweet serenade.

6

It isn't just a tortoise, is it, though?
There's some other sound in it. Some sort of low.

All

Summat's been flayed
for this sweet serenade.

7

Yer, some other sound keeps coming through.
It's more than a tortoise. It's got like a *moo*.

All

Summat's been flayed
for this sweet serenade.

And the question is
to this kid that's a whiz
where did you get that gut?

Them leather thongs
he twangs into songs
to comfort, or, maybe, carouse,
we don't have to go through
the whole bloody zoo
they come from Apollo's nicked cows.

(KYLLENE *is tipped off the stage. her pediment falls. Four*
SATYRS *try to lift it. They can't.* KYLLENE *raises it again with*
effortless Olympic lift. Exits with as much dignity as possible.)

KYLLENE

ως απολλυμαι κακως . . . O woe! O woe!
I'm not in the right play. I'd better go.

45

(Exit tragedy pursued by a SATYR.*)*

CHORUS OF SATYRS

1

Well, we've found Apollo's cattle. We'll be freed.
He'll give us some gold to buy all we need.

2

And that *we* need's not some plaything to pluck.
Satyrs need to get drunk and then fuck.

All

APOLLO! APOLLO! APOLLO!

(Enter APOLLO *from the rear screen. He is calling mournfully after his cows using their pet Greek names:)*

APOLLO

Κανελλω μου . . . Ασπρουλα μου . . . Παρδαλω μου . . .
Λενιω μου . . . Αρχοντα μου . . . Μαρυουλα μου . . .
Αστηρης μου . . .

Where are my loved ones, give them to me,
then I'll give you the gold and set you all free.

SATYR 1

You have to face up to it, sir, this 'lyre'
's all you've got left of the bulls from your byre.

SATYR 2

The strings of this thing came from your herd's guts
and these were the horns that waved, once, on their
    nuts.

SATYR 3

And look at this, squire, this membrane of hide.
Bet it came off a flayed bullock's backside.

46

SATYR 4

Them lovely moo-cows you mooned over, squire.
All that's left of the lot is this little lad's lyre.

SATYR 5

Sorry to tell you but this little lad
's squeezed all your steers into t'prototype Strad.

SATYR 6

We've tracked them the length and breadth of the land
And now all they're fit for's to play in a band.

SATYR 7

Your cows have been kaputted by this kid.
She says he's called Hermes, this Caryatid.

SATYR 8

She claims he's her charge, claims she's his nurse
and insists on spouting Victorian verse.

SATYR 9

She's called Kyllene, or so she claims
but I think they're both of 'em assumed names.

SATYR 10

This crappy little chappy we apprehended
she claims that he's Zeus-descended.

SATYR 11

You're a god, squire. Is he one or not?
Does he strike you as one of your lot?

SATYR 12

I'll wager my share of the spoil this widdling wain's
not got a drop of god's blood in his veins.

APOLLO

He'll have to be quizzed this whiz-kid you've tracked

and you'll be rewarded, as per our pact.
This bovver babe, this bovicidal maniac.
I'll beat him black and blue to get my bulls back.
I'll skin the bugger. I'll do him in.
I'll make a drum from the little sod's skin.

(*Fluctuates between rage and grief and fascination with the sounds the guts of his pets now send into the air about him.*)

Fetch him out. Fetch him out. He'll feel my fist
this infant . . . instrumentalist . . .

CHORUS OF SATYRS
Fetch him out! Fetch him out! Fetch him out!

(*The* SATYRS *begin a 'Fetch him out!' chant like 'Here we go' and also stamp a rhythm on the platforms. It reaches a crescendo and there is a silence and expectation in which* APOLLO *repeats his threat.*)

APOLLO
Fetch him out. Fetch him out. He'll feel my fist
this infant . . . instrumentalist . . .

(*Enter from the gap in the papyrus a large* HERMES *in a nappy made of papyrus scraps. He terrifies* APOLLO *who backs off at great speed. The projection of the baby disappears just before* HERMES *enters.* APOLLO *has retreated almost to the expedition tent.*)

Hermes, whiz-kid, son of Zeus and Maia,
You're the thief who stole my herd from the byre
and dehorned and degutted they went into your lyre.

HERMES
How can you say that? Herd? Herd? Herd?
I'm only five days old. I've never heard the word.
Until that is you come here and them and holler

that I'm the one that stole the cattle of Apollo.
Never heard of 'herd'. No, sorry, pet,
'herd' isn't even in my lexicon yet.
I'm still trying to learn the alphabet.
This is my lyre. This is my invention.
Listen to its magic. Everybody! Pay attention!

(HERMES *begins to play the lyre so beautifully and melodiously that angry* APOLLO *and the threatening, advancing* SATYRS *are charmed into listening. At the end of the recital* APOLLO *is sufficiently charmed to want the lyre in exchange for his cut-up cattle.*)

APOLLO
Fellow immortal, son of Zeus and Maia,
I beg you to teach me the art of the lyre.
This was all fated. I feel that it was meant
to create for my sole use this soothing instrument.

(APOLLO *tries to snatch the lyre from* HERMES.)

HERMES
Gerroff my lyre. I made it. It's mine.

APOLLO
But I'm older than you, and a lot more divine.
Give me your gadget. Be a good boy!
I could give class to your trivial toy.

HERMES
It's boring for a baby in his cradle all day.
I'd go proper potty with no lyre to play.

APOLLO
Let me have your gadget or you'll get a good slap.
That papyrus you're wearing. It's full of warm crap.

That nymph's too snooty to change a kid's nappy.
I can't help it, can I, if I'm all crappy.

(HERMES *sobs*.)

APOLLO
There, there, little fellow, but you're scarcely fit
to give lyre recitals with pants full of shit.
You're frankly disgusting. I think that the lyre
requires a performer in formal attire.
Change your crappy papyrus while I serenade
these lowly satyrs with the lyre you made.

(*Prepares to play and as he plucks the lyre he hears one of his lost cows in the seven strings*.)

[1] Pluck . . . Κανελλω μου . . .
[2] Pluck . . . Παρδαλω μου . . .
[3] Pluck . . . Αρχονρα μου . . .
[4] Pluck . . . Αστηρης μου . . .

[5] Pluck . . . Ασπουλα μου . . .
[6] Pluck . . . Λενιω μου . . .
[7] Pluck . . . Μαρυουλα μου . . .

(*The* μου/*moo at the end of each name is echoed by 'mooings' in the air*.)

The elements that made our drama live
might seem, on first appearance, negative.
Deserts, a papyrus torn to tatters,
theft, a trail of turds, and sniffing satyrs . . .
From that unpromising, unlikely start
from barrenness and turds we have brought art,
and art that draws together and transcends
the boundaries of nations and makes friends.
This mottled tortoise, this creeping thing

50

joined to my cattle makes dumb Nature sing.
Some comfort, maybe, knowing that my herd's
gone into a gadget more soothing than mere words.
Debeeved, bereaved, I almost can rejoice
that was dead and dumb now has a voice.

The gods decreed a fixed scale in creation
from the Olympian, like me, to the crustacean,
and almost at the bottom of the scale,
even below your sort with hoof and tail,
and tail-bearers with no part human, come
creatures like this tortoise who are dumb.
The scale of creation like a scale with notes
runs the whole gamut from gods to goats,
and distinctly closer to the latter,
low on the scale of being, comes the satyr,
earthbound in the way you dance and drink,
goatish in your instinct and your stink.
You're almost at the bottom but not quite.
Below the beasts, all beast, come beetles and the mite
whose mandibles make meals of Sophocles
and leave gaping holes in such lost plays as these.
This little mite, the lowest in creation
turns Sophocles to dust and defecation,
and turns manuscripts of Mankind's masterpieces
to little microbe meals and microbe faeces,
letters, then a line, a page of words
made minutest mincemeat and the tiniest of turds.
The gods decreed that transformation
was a basic principle in all creation.
The preferred direction's lower into higher
like the tortoise turned into this lyre,
a process that the desert mite reverses
every time he snacks on buried verses.

CHORUS OF SATYRS

I

It's very sad, though, the tortoise had to die.

As part goat or horse, I part identify.

2

When Nature gets made use of for Man's needs
my heart, at least the horse part of me, bleeds.

3

But when I see the outcome, all the rest
of me, the two-thirds human, is impressed.

4

One part wonders. One part identifies.
And both parts bring the tears into my eyes.

5

I greet the gadget of the gutted shell
but grieve for the deroofed animal as well.

6

We've got hoofs of horn. He might have killed us
and sold our hoofs and guts to banjo-builders.

7

Odd how we're always in things at the start –
the creation of fire, the lyre, wine and art.

8

We're envoys of Nature who give their consent
to surrender the substance they use to invent.

9

Woodlands for barbecues, pressed grapes for wine
but where should a satyr start drawing the line?

10

Since fire first came to earth the charcoal-makers
have bulldozed down Arcadia's bosky acres.

II

The leafy bushes we used to quaff and screw in
the barbecuing craze brought into ruin.

I2

The dryads undergo decortication
and retreat from reservation to reservation.

I

Always in retreat, moved on yet again
outside the pale of lyre-playing men.

2

They're encouraged by the consent of us man/horses
in their exploitation of Earth's natural resources.

3

Ay, and I ought to confess to being a quick consentor
to grapes being crushed for wine by its inventor.

4

When Dionysos started giving wine away
the horse part of the satyr never said *neigh*.

5

Witnessing wine, I formed the intention
of witnessing every year its re-invention.

APOLLO

And soon you'll be free to drink till you fall,
the freedom it seems that you want most of all.
But first let's find a name to honour the creatures
who died to give the lyre its essential features.
The cattle and the tortoise that had to die
should give this thing a name we'll call it by.
The future should be able to deduce
its animal origin from χελων and βους
To honour gut and shell that give its tone

53

I hereby call this thing the *boucelloniphone*.

1
But we should honour more than these two.
What about us satyrs who ran it to ground?

2
We're allus excluded when t'honours come round.

3
What about *satyro*boucelloniphone?

APOLLO
*Apollo*satyroboucelloniphone!

SILENUS
(*suddenly appearing but as though he'd been there all the time*)

Apollo*sileno*satyroboucellon-
and-all-the-bloody-rest-i-phone!

APOLLO
Let's go back to 'lyre' and forget the whole zoo.
And *now* the reward that I promised you.
A reward for you satyrs and for you lot out there
is to listen to the lyre's world première.

(APOLLO *takes up the lyre and plays a beautiful melody.*
The SATYRS *are genuinely and deeply enraptured by the*
melody. So much so that when APOLLO *has finished his recital*
the SATYRS *crowd round and want to have a turn with the*
instrument.)

SATYR I
Oh, it's wonderful. Let me have a go!
I'd love to try it out.

54

APOLLO

(*Suddenly very angry*)

NO! NO! NO!
My advice is stick to being satyrs
and don't go meddling with musical matters.
You don't need lyres. You're natural celebrators
stuck between animal and human status.
You need no consolations of high art –
your human pain's cancelled by your horse/goat part.
You don't need lyres. Your days proceed
from one need satisfied to the next need.
And because, as satyrs, you're grossly oversexed
the next succeeds the next succeeds the next.
The gratification of all sensual need,
the horny stallion and the randy steed,
the rhythm of your hoofs, your stamp and strut,
have no need of these seven strings of gut.
You're satyrs, remember. You don't need lyres
while your goat parts tether you to brute desires.
When the man part of you feels a human pain
the goat part puts you on your hoofs again.
When a satyr's human part feels human woes
the gee-gee in him just gees up and goes.
Your capers and your clogs' staccato clatters –
exactly the racket expected of satyrs.

I'm Apollo, inspirer, appreciator
of artist, musician and creator.
Tell the truth it didn't suit a god
the cowpoke's lariat and cattle prod.
I'm not a cowherd really. It's more me
the sphere of music and of poetry.
This is now *my* lyre and I define
its music as half-human, half-divine.
And satyrs, I repeat, must not aspire
in any way to mastering my lyre.

Do you need reminding how I had to flay
your brother Marsyas *pour encourager*
and I hereby have to warn all *les autres*
not to touch or try playing one note.

(*The* SATYRS, *already saddened both by the melody and then
by* APOLLO*'s speech, are totally terrified and devastated by his
reminding them of Marsyas, the satyr flayed alive by* APOLLO
*for mastering the flute, newly invented then discarded by
Athene.*)

But I have to grant that you sniffed out the track
and got me what's left of my cattle back.
You kept your promise. My cattle got tracked.
You'll get what I promised as per our pact –
gold and freedom. You're free, if you stay
within the strict form of the satyr play.
Gold and freedom – here's gold. And you're free
so long as you stay here in Arcady.

(APOLLO *plays his lyre while* KYLLENE *comes from the tent
and hands out large gold bars, one to each* SATYR.)

So much for you lot. And as for me
I'm a god, and I'll always be free.
I'm off to compose a new paean or ode
in my very own temple just down the road.

(*Exit* APOLLO *to the Temple of Apollo.* APOLLO *makes the
long exit towards the rear screen with the projection of Apollo
from the Delphi plate now plus the lyre. The* CHORUS OF
SATYRS *are thoroughly cowed. They line up for the 'rewards'
of gold which* APOLLO *had pulled out of a crate. They are like
children lining up for Santa Claus only they have no excitement
at what they receive. Each of the 'gold bars' is in fact a
'ghetto-blaster' wrapped in gold foil. The* SATYRS *sit in a curve
following the rim of the stadium and open their 'presents' in a
half-hearted, sad way, and grumbling as they do. When they*

open them they have no idea what they are. The confrontation is like one of those supposedly amusing accounts of say, Africans or Indians first seeing some gadget of 'white man's civilization', and sometimes they are like Cheetah in the Tarzan films getting hold of a camera, or mirror or telephone.)

CHORUS OF SATYRS

1

Who wants some stupid tortoise to strum?

2

He can stick his bloody banjo up his bum!

3

Once it gains a foothold in our habitat
with its plinkety-plonk, well, that'll be that.

4

It'll be in t'woods, in t'hills, grass, t'air –

5

Ay, even in t'toilet and that's everywhere.

6

Every cave, every grot, every bosky retreat
'll soon be throbbing with Apollo's lyre beat.

7

Plucking piped out from morn till eve.
Here'll be unliveable. We'll all have to leave.

8

There'll be no stretch of sky, no bit of ground
that won't in the end be full of its sound.

9

When Hermes took cow-gut and tortoise-shell
did he know that he'd turn our peace into hell?

57

You watch what'll happen. It'll force the poor birds .
out of business. You mark my words.

As songsters that is. It'll still be their fate
to stew in rich sauces for some human's plate.

It'll usurp the susurrations . . .

The who?

The rustles, the whispers, the tu-whit and tu-whoo.

The repertoire of rapture, the moan
of doves, the murmur of innumerable bees.

The rustling of dresses of dryades,
their stockingtops purring as their thighs
rub together . . .

the buzz of bluebottles and flies.

Ay, birdsong's *passé*. This lyre'll usurp.
the song of the skylark, the cricket's chirp.

Eventually everything's going to get drowned
in such all-surrounding and man-made sound.

8

Don't like it at all. It'll come to no good
letting such loud din loose in the wood.

9

This lyre contraption's the thin end of the wedge.
We'll soon have this Muzak behind every hedge.

10

The beginning of the end. You wait and see,
There'll be plinkety-plonk from every damned tree.

(*By this time the* CHORUS OF SATYRS *have opened all their
'presents'. The ghetto-blasters lie on the ground in front of them
forming a curve. Suddenly, very loudly, the ghetto-blasters begin
to play the same melody as* APOLLO *played during his lyre
recital, but deafening rock-style. The* SATYRS *try to dance to it,
can't and in a panic at the sound they flee to the rear screen.*
SILENUS *is left alone to face the unbearable chorus of ghetto-
blasters. One by one he smashes them into silence. When the
echoes have died away he speaks seriously to the audience.*)

SILENUS

Civilization! Once man starts on that track
even for a satyr there's no going back.
The 'boucelloniphone', Apollo's lyre
leads, by leaps and bounds, to the amplifier,
the guts of cows and the tortoise-shell
to steel-plucked deafening decibel.

(*Lights a brazier and wraps a papyrus 'cloak' round himself.*)

Papyrus to codex, book to film and tape
once they're invented then there's no escape.
And fire, that takes the bleak chill off the night
could, if men don't watch it, set the world alight.
Disco descends directly from his lyre
and global holocaust from cosy fire.

59

The glowing grills where *kokkoretsi* turns
grow to conflagrations where the whole globe burns.

(*Looks, finds the moon.*)

The moon hymned for aeons by love-sick hacks
is already pock-marked with spaceboot tracks.
Tracks no earthbound, earth-loving satyr wants to
    follow
though that waste above's been visited by Apollo.
When the world seems hurtling in the wrong direction
remember the satyr with his wineskin and erection.

(*Regards his own limp appendage.*)

Sorry to say so but that's a side
of satyrdom the lads have to provide.
My time for tupping's done as you can see.
No maenad's moist μουνάκι opens now for me.

But a satyr, good people, doesn't just exist
solely for fucking or for getting pissed.
We're not just the clowns sent in to clear the ring
we're here to show surprise at everything.
We satyrs are on hand to reassess
from basic principles all you possess,
to show reactions apparently naive
to what you take for granted or believe.
To ask the simple wherefore, why, and what,
to show, for the first time ever, fire's hot.
We're sort of guinea-pigs for gadgets, fire,
the sculptural likeness, this new-fangled lyre.
Of all the gadgets we were required to test
this gadget made from grape juice suits me best.

We're all served our time with that weight on our heads
But no satyr ever trod where tragedy treads
Gods, kings, and heroes have all walked there.

High and low divided just by a stair
Now's my big chance! Do I dare, do I dare!

(*Spotlight on papyrus.*)

   . . . ως απολλυμαι κακως . . . O woe, O woe.

(*Enter* SILENUS *through papyrus.*)

Not bad for a satyr for his first go!

Satyrs in theatre are on hand to reassess
doom and destiny and dire distress.
Six hours of tragedy and half an hour of fun.
But they were an entity conceived as one.
But when the teachers and critics made their selections
they elbowed the satyrs with embarrassing erections.
Those teachers of tragedy sought to exclude
the rampant half-animals as offensive and rude.
But whose eyes first beheld the Promethean blaze?

(*In answer comes the shouted response of the* CHORUS OF
SATYRS *supported also by the 'ghosts' of the 8000 spectators at
the ancient Pythian Games.*)

CHORUS

Ours!

SILENUS

(*Shouting back*)

And whose horse-lugs hear the first lyre when it plays?

CHORUS

Ours!

SILENUS

And who kissed the flames and found they were hot?

US!

SILENUS
And who saw their ugly mugs first fashioned in pot?

CHORUS
US!

SILENUS
And when the first vintage was picked from the vine,
Who watched it ferment, who supped the first wine?

CHORUS
US!

SILENUS
Who pioneered the art of getting pissed?

CHORUS
US!

SILENUS
Who's indispensable to the papyrologist?

CHORUS
US!
Ichneftés. Ichneftés. Ichneftés.

SILENUS
Who scrabbled in sand to find bits of Greek?

CHORUS
US!

SILENUS
Who pulled from oblivion the words that we speak?
US! US! US!

CHORUS
US! US! US!

(SILENUS *allows the echoes of the* CHORUS *and the 8000*
ghosts of the Pythian Games to die away, then continues.)

SILENUS
We have to keep a proper distance though.
We're meant as Calibans to serve a Prospero.
Deferential, rustic, suitably in awe
of new inventions is what your satyr's for.
But we mustn't, as you heard, actually aspire
to actually *play* your actual lyre.
Wondering, applauding, that's our participation
but satyrs have to stick to their satyr station.
Apollo mentioned Marsyas who lost his skin
and all he really wanted was to join in.
Did Marsyas deserve his awful flaying
for a bit of innocent *aulos* playing?
Your satyr's fine in music just as long
he doesn't think that *he* can sing the song.
To be an applauding punter but not to trespass
on cultural preserves like brother Marsyas.

The *aulos* was Athene's flute. She flung it away
so why shouldn't my brother pick it up and play?
After only a few blows the goddess gave the flute
she'd just invented the elegant boot.
She flung the thing aside. Do you know why?
Think of the *aulos*. Ever had a try?
You puff your cheeks out, like this, when you play
and *she* didn't like her face to look that way.

63

She though it unattractive. Well, its true
her cheeks looked like balloons when the goddess blew.
And who should see the flung flute in the grass
but our brother satyr, Marsyas?
Questions of cosmetics scarcely matter
to one who had the ugly mug of a satyr.

It wasn't for good looks that Marsyas was noted
so he blew and blew and let his cheeks get bloated.
He took himself off to a quiet bit of wood
and girned and puffed and grunted and got *good*.
Can't you hear the Muses on Parnassós say
'Who gave a common satyr licence to play?'
Music's an inner circle that has to exclude
from active participation a beast so crude.

'How can *he* be a virtuoso on the flute?
Look at the hoofs on him. He's half a brute!'
His one and only flaw. He showed that flutes
sound just as beautiful when breathed into by 'brutes'.
It confounded the categories of high and low
when Caliban could outplay Prospero.

So the goddess Athene's discarded whistle
turned brother Marsyas to gore and gristle.
And while Marsyas suffered his slow flaying
Apollo looked on with his 'doo-dah' playing.
The last thing that he saw was his own skin
like a garment at his feet with no one in.
Wherever the losers and the tortured scream
the lyres will be playing the Marsyas theme.
You'll hear the lyres playing behind locked doors
where men flay their fellows for an abstract cause.
The kithara cadenza, the Muse's mezzo trill
cover the skinning and the screaming still.

Wherever in the world there is prison and pain
the powerful are playing the Marsyas refrain.

In every dark dungeon where blood has flowed
the lyre accompanies the Marsyas ode.
Wherever the racked and the anguished cry
there's always a lyre-player standing by.
Some virtuoso of Apollo's *Ur*-violin
plays for the skinners as they skin.

And *why* shouldn't Marsyas or me aspire
to be virtuosos of the flute or . . . lyre?

If Marsyas had touched it and said 'ooo'
the way that us satyrs are supposed to do,
but he went and picked it up and blew the flute
and that was trespassing for the man/brute.
For *them* it would have been quite enough
to have given it just one abortive puff,
a buffoonish ballooning of the brutish cheeks
producing a few, and inexpert, squeaks,
that would have amused them and been OK
but Marsyas, man/animal, he learned to *play*.
To have watched him smell it, test it with his teeth
or use it like the pygmies as a penis sheath,
all allowable, all tolerated fun,
but the Apollonian goes for his gun,
when it suddenly dawns on him the swine
the pearl is cast before by one divine
knows it's a pearl, and not some novel food
and aspires beyond dumb swinetude.
When he enters the Culture it represents
they reach for their skin-removing instruments.

They're less accommodating the satyrs of today.
They wouldn't condescend to be in a satyr play.
They've joined the *polis* and they've learned its ways
but they despise its music and its plays.
I'm too used to it here. I'll never lead 'em
into the future with their new-found freedom.
I want to implore them: 'Children, stay

and be satyrs with me and play out this play.'

But they won't listen, and they're on their way
straight through the confines of the stupid satyr play.

(*Enter the new generation of* S A T Y R S. *They are like football
hooligans with scarves, flags, etc., and chanting and clapping.
The* S A T Y R S *spray the name 'Marsyas' (in Greek letters:
Μαρσυασ) first with red, then with white aerosol paints, the
colour of the Greek team Olympiakos. Then they add* Μαρσυασ
*in blue for England. ('Marsyas! Marsyas! Marsyas!') They slash
the papyrus. They spray* Μαρσυασ *in inflammable fuel and set
light to it so that the name of* Μαρσυασ *blazes on the screen
papyrus. They kick the smashed ghetto-blasters into life. They
blare out the 'Marsyas Theme'.*)

That's enough, lads. Leave things as they are.
I may be a satyr. But in there I'm star.

CHORUS OF SATYRS
(*Passing along a torch lit from* S I L E N U S' *brazier and cans of
beer.*)

1
We were the witnesses when the first fire came.

2
We were the first to flinch from the flame.

3
When I kissed the fire it blistered my face.

4
I burned my beard off in that fiery embrace.

5
Yer, we thought the flames lovely and gave 'em a kiss.

66

6

And our beards set alight with a blistering hiss.

7

They used our innocence to play a bad joke.

8

Ever since then my hair's smelled of smoke.

9

It's not just that fact that Marsyas got flayed.

10

There's plenty of tricks the buggers have played.

11

And we connived at the clowning, thought it a way
of getting a hoofhold into a play.

12

We're going to destroy and we're enjoying

1

destroying for the sake of destroying.

2

We're doing the burning, and the bloody lyre
is wired to our turned-up amplifier.

(*Loud beat from ghetto-blaster.*)

3

No more deferential dummies from a satyr play.
From now on MARSYAS RULES OK?

(*Ghetto-blaster beat.*)

If I can't be a man I'll be wholly goat

and stuff the papyrus down Sophocles' throat.

(*Ghetto-blaster beat.*)

4

Fellaheen, phallus-bearers only for farce.
Well, show us a tragedy we'll show you our arse.

5

Aeschylus, Sophocles, gerroff our backs.
We're hijacking Culture and leaving no tracks.

(*The* SATYR *begin to burn down the papyrus of the* Ichneutae.)

SILENUS
Don't burn the papyrus. That's where we come from!

(*They watch the papyrus burn and drink beer and scatter the cans
on the mounds where the papyri were extracted from. These are
the new rubbish mounds of Oxyrhynchus.*)

To them old Silenus is an Uncle Tom.

(*Shouting to* SATYRS)

Don't burn the papyrus. We're all inside.
Don't burn the papyrus. It's satyricide!

CHORUS OF SATYRS
Either fuck off, old feller, or give us a hand.

(SILENUS *stays still.*)
Then fuck off, old feller, back to fairyland.

SILENUS
Apollo promised freedom. And free you now are
but Apollo didn't intend it to go so far.

(*Begins to exit, then stops.*)

> I didn't mind a bit of inferior status
> as long as there was Bacchus to inebriate us.
> I didn't mind a bit of lowly forelock-tugging
> as long as it went with retsina-glugging.
> To social inequality I turned a blind eye
> if that guaranteed the liquor supply.
> Some sort of pattern seemed to exist,
> get a bit pissed on then go and get pissed.
> I didn't mind conniving with gods and their greed
> if my modest wants were guaranteed.
> Unlike my poor flayed brother, Marsyas,
> I never yearned to move out of my class.
> Better we satyrs stay where we are
> with Bacchus at least there's a buckshee bar.

(SILENUS *tries to drink again from his wineskin and finds it empty. He begins to pick over the rubbish mounds for discarded beer cans.*)

> I'm a happy horse/human, half and half.
> Maybe I'd like less hair on my calf,
> my features might be a little less coarse
> more of the human and less of the horse.
> But unlike brother Marsyas I don't aspire
> to master the flute or play on the lyre.
> In short, I suppose, I'm not really averse
> to being a satyr. I could do a lot worse.

(*To* CHORUS)

> So don't make waves, boys. Don't rock the boat.
> And add up the pluses of being man/goat.

(*The* CHORUS OF SATYRS *take no notice, and go about their destruction and scattering of litter.*)

My lads, they're different. They don't agree.
When they call for freedom. They mean *really* free.

(SILENUS *makes a long exit to where the rear screen used to
hang. The destroyed papyri leave two 'goal posts' and the*
CHORUS OF SATYRS *begin a six-aside football match. They
use a rolled-up bundle of papyrus of the* Ichneutae *as their ball,
and then it changes into a real football. The cheer of the ancient
8000 ghosts of the Pythian Games is heard when a goal is scored.
Also earlier chants. We hear again the fragments that began the
play,* APOLLO*'s first words and the first words of the whole play
now going back into oblivion.*)

VOICE OF APOLLO

. . . .]σ[. . .

. . . .]κιο[. . .

. . . .]πειτα[. . .

. . . .]πεσσυϑ[. . .

. . .]γ[. . .]λ[. . . . . .]ω[. . .

(*The final omega is echoed with a huge 'Oh' from the 8000 ghosts
at the Pythian Games. There is the sound like a dying firework of*
Ιχνευτες *off the Phaedriades.*)

(*After the darkness for the curtain call the* CHORUS *run from
the rear screen with blazing torches and a flaming 'World Cup'
which is placed centre stadium. They then rush forward with
torches high and reprise the 'Paean for the People of Delphi',
but this time it is 'sung' not rhythmically chanted.*

They hand their torches to the 'Greek Fellaheen'.

Eight members of the CHORUS *pick up eight scattered crate
lids and hold them up to the audience. They are the eight letters
of the name of* ΣΟΦΟΚΛΗΣ *but in the wrong order. The
remaining four* CHORUS *reprise a little of the clog dance.*

GRENFELL *and* HUNT *enter from the rear screen with
electric torches searching.*

*With the help of the audience they rearrange the letters held up
by the* CHORUS *so that they read the name of Sophocles.*

ΣΟΦΟΚΛΗΣ

This is the curtain call of Sophocles.

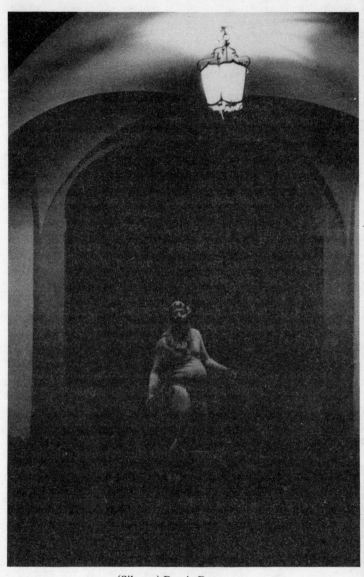

(Silenus) Barrie Rutter
backstage in Vienna

THE NATIONAL THEATRE TEXT

Rehearsals at Saltaire

Rehearsal at Art Carnuntum

This version of *The Trackers of Oxyrhynchus* was first
performed at the Olivier Theatre on 27 March 1990, with the
following company:

GRENFELL/APOLLO	Jack Shepherd
HUNT/SILENUS	Barrie Rutter
KYLLENE	Edna Dore
HERMES	Brian Glover
CHORUS OF FELLAHEEN/SATYRS	Mark Addy
	Peter Andrew
	Christopher Beck
	Stephen Bent
	Colin R. Campbell
	Neil Caple
	Lawrence Evans
	Billy Fellows
	Jack Hardy
	Simon Rackman
	Peter Thorogood
	Andy Wear
PALE BOY	Lawrence Evans
Director	Tony Harrison
Designer	Jocelyn Herbert
Composer	Stephen Edwards
Lighting	Paul McLeish
Laktismography	Lawrence Evans
Music Director	Peter Thorogood
Musicians	Martin Allen
	(MD/percussion)
	Michael Gregory
	(percussion)
Staff Director	Frank Nealon
Production Manager	Andrew Peat
Stage Manager and Director's Assistant	Trish Montemuro
Deputy Stage Managers	David Curl
	Angela Fairclough

Assistant Stage Managers	Steven Dexter
	Valerie Fox
Sound	Paul Arditti
	Christopher Shutt
Designer's Assistant	Vicki Hallam
Design Assistant	Annie Gosney

Three Satyrs. Left to right Christopher Beck, Simon
Rackham and Jack Hardy

As the audience take their seats we see FELLAHEEN *working in the trenches and on the mounds of the ancient rubbish tips of Oxyrhynchus. As if from the very horizon of the desert, we hear the low, protracted sigma of the first fragmentary letter of the* Ichneutae *of Sophocles. Only* GRENFELL *hears it.* HUNT *and the* FELLAHEEN *hear nothing. The sigma makes* GRENFELL *agitated and he transfers his agitation to the* FELLAHEEN. *He intercepts a* FELLAH *with a papyrus in his hand making the regular journey from excavation trench to table outside the expedition tent, where* HUNT *is writing labels for the full crates.*

GRENFELL

O what's Arabic for *gently*? Gently, please!
You might have in your grubby paws the soul of
   Sophocles!

(GRENFELL *takes the papyrus from the* FELLAH.)

You've got to keep these people on their toes!

(*Glances at papyrus.*)

I can tell at a glance it's another bit of prose.
Another cap-in-hand petition to go with those.

(*Drops papyrus into crate labelled petitions.*
HUNT *retrieves papyrus from crate to log it, then puts it back again.*)

HUNT

Grenfell, I love literature quite as much as you
but these petitions have historical and human interest
   too.

GRENFELL

I wish they could work faster, I really do!

But we've almost filled eight crates since the crack of
    dawn
and if they work too fast the papyri all get torn.
We set ourselves a quota of nine full crates a day.

GRENFELL

And all of them petitions, not a scrap of poem or play!

(*Carts are about to be hauled away.*)

Better label that lot before they're hauled away.

We won't get very far at this Egyptian speed.
And those crates are all petitions from people in need.
Why can't we find a masterpiece that lifts the soul to
    read?

(*Lids are hammered on to full crates, which* HUNT *labels and
numbers before they are towed away.*)

GRENFELL

We're 'Trackers', *Ichneutae*, and what we seek
are fragments of papyri in ancient Greek.
These boxes being loaded will soon be shipped
from Egypt back to Oxford where we work on the
    script.
First we dig, then we decipher, then we must
deduce the missing letters mouldered into dust.
And when we fail to fathom what comes next
we put brackets to show there's a gap in the text.
And a gap in a text is like a bottomless pit
and one sometimes feels one's falling into it.

Here at Oxyrhynchus where there's never been much
    rain
are rubbish heaps of riches. All these mounds contain
preserved papyri from the distant past.

The papyri potential of all these heaps is vast!
These mounds need excavating fast. Fast! Fast!

Rubbish heaps of riches! Quite a paradox!
Each papyrus goes in its labelled box,
in this, say, wage-bills for labour on a road
and in this, say, fragments of a Sapphic Ode.
This, piles of petitions from waifs and strays,
that, precious papyri of poetry and plays.
To all this ancient rubbish, each waste papyrus tip
Hunt and I apply our Oxford scholarship.
This chaos and confusion Hunt and I
are called upon by fate to try to classify
and that struggle commences right here with our crates
a crudish filing system that facilitates
further refinements back in Oxford where
the papyri can be given the best specialist care.

(*Sees* FELLAH *fumbling a papyrus out of corner of his eye.*)

Not the kind of treatment they're being given over
    there!

(GRENFELL *rescues papyrus, glances at it, only a petition.*)

The past is rubbish till scholars take the pains
to sift and sort and interpret the remains.
This chaos is the past, mounds of heaped debris
just waiting to be organized into history.

(*To* FELLAHEEN)

Yes, and all together, heave!

(*To audience*)

One can't be ever off the strict *qui vive*!

79

The desert! The desert can do a person in
unless one imposes the strictest discipline
and part of the discipline that I impose
is having all our boxes divided into rows.

GRENFELL
The strictest schedule, an almost military routine
to organize our otherwise unruly Fellaheen.
That behaviour over there shows you what I mean!

(*Flurry of unruly behaviour from* FELLAHEEN *in trench.*)

These chaps, our Fellaheen, can't see what's unique
about scraps of old papyri in ancient Greek.
We ship back papyri and decipher them at Queen's
but the natives used to use them as compost for their
    greens!
These treasures of a soul-enriching ancient tongue
shovelled on to barrows and used like so much dung!
Just imagine Homer, Sophocles and Plato
used as compost for the carrot and potato.
They even burn papyrus for the fragrance it releases
and fumigate their fetid tents with long-lost masterpieces!

Papyri! Insects gnaw them. Time corrodes
and native plants get potted in a mulch of Pindar's Odes.
Horrible to contemplate! How can a person sleep
while Sophocles is rotting on an ancient rubbish heap?

Here at Oxyrhynchus our present excavation's
lived up to and surpassed all expectations.
Crate after crate shipped off, load after load
from laundry list and ledger work to tragedy and ode.
Though I'm peeved to report so far this expedition's
pretty short on poetry but piles up these petitions.

HUNT
We have both become obsessive. So many loads per hour

before they end up compost on some Cairo cauliflower.
But with a family of infant Fellaheen to feed
manure for the cabbage patch must seem the greater
   need.
But we have to be manic not to slip behind
digging and deciphering and logging each new find.

(*Voice of* APOLLO *from the desert.*
GRENFELL *out of tent again, then back in.*)

(*Confiding*)

> Grenfell gets so anxious to find dramatic scraps
> it almost brought the poor chap close to a collapse.
> Grenfell's fast at everything. He can actually *read*
> what most people can't decipher, at incredible speed.
> Grenfell's electrical, so mercurial and quick
> I often fear the work will make my old friend sick.
> Grenfell's torrential, so dazzlingly fast
> I sometimes fear his sanity might not last.
> I worry about Grenfell. Only last year
> he said the god Apollo was shouting in his ear.
> Apollo pursuing him, Grenfell couldn't rest
> till he became, I fear to say, quite literally possessed.
> He viewed the way our names were in conjunction
> Grenfell-Hunt as an Apollonian injunction.
> He heard Apollo yammering for scraps and tatters
> of a lost play of Sophocles: *The Tracking Satyrs*.
> 'Grenfell, Hunt!' he heard the voice abjure,
> 'prevent Apollo's favourite play becoming mere
>   manure.'
> Night and day the voice went: 'Grenfell, Bernard Pine,
> hunt for my papyrus. This order is divine!'

(FELLAHEEN *activity up.*
GRENFELL *from tent to table.* GRENFELL *and* HUNT
sorting papyri from baskets brought by FELLAHEEN.)

81

GRENFELL

Petition from someone poor and alone
petition appealing for . . . moan . . . moan . . .
    moan . . .

HUNT

(*Half-speed, writing*)

Petition from someone poor and alone
petition appealing for shelter or a loan.

GRENFELL

Letter on beer-tax to the ταραχευται 'mummifiers'.

HUNT

But ταραχευται might mean 'salt-fish suppliers'.

GRENFELL

It might! It might! It might! It might!
God! I do wish some *literature* would come to light!

(*We hear from the desert the fragments of the* Ichneutae, *spoken
by* APOLLO/(GRENFELL).)

Did you hear that? That faraway moan?

HUNT

Take a rest, Bernard. I can manage alone.

GRENFELL

(*Huffed and back to deciphering*)

Acknowledgement of loan of vegetable seed
and . . . and . . . and . . . the rest I can't read.

(GRENFELL *hands papyrus to* HUNT. HUNT *studies it and
deciphers*.)

HUNT

Sale of donkey . . . 56 Drachs!

GRENFELL

Receipt for payment of cattle-tax . . .

Petition, petition, Ptolemaic 2 A D . . .
and . . . and . . . and . . . now let me see
letter from Gemellius . . . (in terrible condition)
Seems to be some sort of . . .

HUNT

Petition!

(GRENFELL *pushes the unsorted basket towards* HUNT. *He has had enough petitions and wants plays.* HUNT *sorts.* GRENFELL *logs.*)

Petition, petition, petition, again
so many petitions from homeless men.
Petition, petition, petition, the same
so many appeals in pity's name.
Petition, petition, more, more, more . . .

GRENFELL

O hardly the papyri we are desperate for!

HUNT

Petitions to some proconsul sent from Rome
not to be evicted from their Oxyrhynchus home.
μη μετάναστης . . . . . . μη λειμω συναπολυμαι.

GRENFELL

Apollo!

HUNT

No, συναπολυμαι 'Don't let me die!'
λειμω . . . 'of hunger' . . . it's quite a constant cry

83

with μη μεταναστης . . . 'Don't make me homeless,
  please!'
So many petitions!

GRENFELL
          And not much Sophocles!
You sort out your ancient waifs and strays
and I'll concentrate my energy on poetry and plays.

HUNT
μεταναστης . . . meaning 'vagrant', 'outcast', 'stray',
Do you realize how many times we've read that phrase
  today?

GRENFELL
Too damned many! Not a scrap of poem or play!
I'm of the opinion that such a flat prosaic plea
simply can't compete with the power of poetry.
It's tragic poetry, not this petitioners' prose,
that makes the woes of ancient sufferers still seem
  woes.
The pain of Hecuba goes on being pain
though we keep returning to it time and time again
but μη μεταναστης soon seems a dull refrain.
μη μεταναστης despite its desperate pleading
rather dies on one after the first reading.

HUNT
Petitions, petitions, petitions against eviction.
They lived in fear, it seems, of homeless dereliction.
That μη μεταναστης 'Don't make me homeless' phrase
shows that we are burrowing into quite appalling days.
And those poor petitioners would all have been
the dispossessed precursors of our present Fellaheen.
Here must have been full of folk in dire need.

GRENFELL
I wonder if your bureaucrat had anything to read.

HUNT

I'm sure that the bureaucrat who read *my* pleas
(as you're pleased to call them) read your Sophocles.
He considered these petitions, then at night
he read our classics by cosy oil-lamplight,
while out in the desert those he'd dispossessed
in no way disturbed his reading or his rest.

(HUNT *has lit the oil-lamp on the table. The* FELLAHEEN
have downed tools and are praying to Mecca.)

GRENFELL

And as a papyrologist I much prefer
papyrus poetry and plays to papyrus *cris-de-coeur*.
In those anxious moments when one unglues
reluctantly twinned pages and one has to choose
between, say, Pindar and some desperate pauper's plea
I'd plump without a second thought for the poetry.
The poor are always with us but the ancient Greek
who gave the world *King Oedipus* will always be unique.

(*Again we hear the first fragments of the* Ichneutae *in the voice of*
APOLLO/(GRENFELL). *Only* GRENFELL *hears it.*)

Did you hear that, like someone's death throes.
A quite unearthly cry from far away?

HUNT

I think you need rest. Go inside for a doze.
I think that it's time to pack in for the day.
Don't want you laid up. I'll manage things here.
Don't want you laid up like you were last year.
I'll see to dismissing the Fellaheen.
If we keep them after dark there'll be an awful scene.
You know our Egyptian will only work by day
and they expect backsheesh once we've seen them pray.

(*The* FELLAHEEN *have lined up after their prayers to receive*

their daily backsheesh. The line-up is like the one we will see
when the SATYRS *are rewarded by* APOLLO. HUNT *pays out.*
The FELLAHEEN *begin to depart.*)

GRENFELL

No! No! No! No!
I don't want all of you to go.
Have you forgotten what I always say.
Get the boxes ready for the break of day.
I want another nine boxes on their spot
so we can start at daybreak *on the dot*.

HUNT

I'm awfully sorry, Grenfell, old chap.
But unlike you I need a little nap.

GRENFELL

(*Confiding to audience*)

I worry about Arthur, I sometimes think
He slips into the tent for a surreptitious drink.

(*To* FELLAHEEN)

Daybreak! Daybreak! Is that clear?
At the first sign of sun I want you all back here.

(GRENFELL *is alone with the lamp at the table outside the tent.*
He is sorting a basket of papyri far more quickly and with less
care than he did in HUNT'*s presence.*)

Census, petition, more stuff of that sort.
Judicial proceedings, minutes of the court . . .

O, what's that? Something that I almost missed,
the verso of that Oxyrhynchus census list.

(*Pause to decipher*)

86

O it's Pindar, Pindar . . . but not all there,
after all those petitions I was beginning to despair.
A paean by Pindar hitherto unknown . . .
Καστaλιας . . . . Απολλωνος . . . . . ϑαμινα Δελφων!
A paean by Pindar hitherto unknown.
A hymn to Apollo lost till this minute.
Castalia . . .
            APOLLO!

GRENFELL/APOLLO
            Thank God I'm in it.

(GRENFELL *is horrified that the voice of* APOLLO *came out of
his mouth. When he cried* APOLLO *the papyrus fell and the
projection of* APOLLO *from the Delphi plate appeared. The
fragments of the first lines of the* Ichneutae *fill the air.*)

            VOICE OF APOLLO
. . .]σ[. . .
. . . .]κιο[. . .
. . . .]πειτα[. . .
. . . .]πεσσυϑ[. . .
. . . . . .]γ[. . . . .]λ[. . .
. . . .]ω[. . .

(GRENFELL *begins a frantic dialogue with himself as both*
GRENFELL *and* APOLLO.)

            GRENFELL
            Apollo
That Paean was fine and full of my praises
but I want that play where I speak the phrases.
            Grenfell
But I'm working as fast as I possibly can!
            Apollo
I suppose that you are, being only a man.

87

Grenfell

Please leave me alone. Please, please go away.

Apollo

I'll pursue you until you track down my play.

Grenfell

I promise. I promise. Now get out of my mind.

Apollo

No, till you find it I'll stay right behind.

Grenfell

I have a pistol, Apollo. I might have to shoot.

Apollo

And you might just regret that, Grenfell, old fruit.
Find the papyrus and fill in the gaps.

Grenfell

I'm working too hard. I'm damned near to collapse.
Do you realize how much time we require?

Apollo

Do *you* realize I require my lyre?
Remember Cassandra. I brought her to heel.

Grenfell

I wouldn't have thought that I had her appeal.

Apollo

Don't be too sure! Just keep on the track
and remember Apollo's right at your back.
Somewhere there's a play where I come on first.

Grenfell

Stop it! Stop it! My brain's going to burst!
Such literary finds are regrettably few.

Apollo

Bernard, old boy, I'm counting on you.

Grenfell

(*Producing papyrus from crate*)

I've found this one. Will this one do?

Apollo

If I get a part or a mention or two.

Grenfell

It's a poem praising Theon from 3 A D .

Apollo

Praising Theon! What about me?

Grenfell

Where, may I ask, did you study your Greek?

Apollo

What's dead to you, dear, I actually speak.
I know Greek a damn sight better than you.
επτατονον χειρεσσι . . . shall I construe?

(*Reads Greek rapidly*)

> επτατονον χειρεσσι λυρην πολυηχεα κρουων
> την αυτος τα πρωτα καμες παρα ποσσι τεκουσης
> 'The lyre in exchange for the bulls of Apollo' . . .
> The rest's difficult Greek that you might not follow.

Grenfell

Almost an alpha! I think that you pass.

Apollo

You'll get gamma minus rammed up your arse!
But you know very well that this fragment won't do.
There's not enough of it. I'm mute and the 'you'
isn't *me* that the poem's lines extoll.
I want the *Ichneutae* and want it made whole.
It's not a piece that you scholars know
so just for starters some fragments go:
απαντα χρηστα . . .

Grenfell

Go to hell!

HUNT

(*From inside tent*)

Bernard! Are you all right? Are you feeling unwell?

89

I'm fine! I'm fine! I'm fine! I'm fine!
Making sure tomorrow's crates are put in proper line.
I asked the Fellaheen to bring another nine.

Apollo

Bernard! You'd better discover that play of mine.

(APOLLO *now taunts* GRENFELL *with more fragments of the lost play the god is seeking.*)

]αξ[. . . . . .]λιθι[. . . . . .]στρ[. . . . . .]μηπ[. . .

Grenfell

Leave me alone. You must let me sleep.

Apollo

. . .]αρου[. . . . . .]ουα[. . . . . .]ροτ[. . . . . .
]ρια[. . .

Grenfell

Go away! Leave me. Get away from here!

Apollo

. . .]λει[. . . . . .]γ[. . . . . .]φλεβο[. . . . . .]μη[. . .

Grenfell

Lost! Lost! In the limbo of history!

Apollo

. . .]ατημε[. . . . . .]ονιου β[. . . . . .]μη φυ[. . .

Grenfell

I'm doing the utmost a mere mortal can do.

Apollo

απαντα χρηστα και . . . . . . something . . . . . . λειν . . .

Grenfell

Stop it! I can't get that phrase from my brain.

Apollo

απαντα χρηστα και . . . . . . something . . . . . . λειν . . .

Grenfell

Stop it! Stop it! You'll drive me insane!

Apollo

απαντα χρηστα και . . . . . . something . . . . . . λειν . . .

Grenfell

I beg you, I beg you. Don't say that again.

(APOLLO *changes the fragment for a moment.*)

Apollo

. . .]σ[. . .] κιο [. . . . . .] πειτα [. . .]πεσσυϑ[. . .
]γ[. . .]λ[. . . . . .]ω[. . .

What goes in the gaps? Come on, Grenfell, you know!

Grenfell

I don't! I don't. Go! Go! Go!

Apollo

απαντα χρηστα και . . . . . . something . . . λειν
You've got to make use of that Queen's College brain
to put all my missing letters in.
From this instant I'm in you and using your skin.

. . .]σ[. . .]κιο[. . . . . .]πειτα[. . . . . .]πεσσυϑ[
. . .]γ[. . .]λ[. . . . . .]ω[. . .

(APOLLO *repeats this fragment again and again until*
GRENFELL *shoots his pistol at* 'APOLLO'. *The projection
disappears from the papyrus. The* FELLAHEEN *rush in and
start setting up the nine boxes.*)

VOICE OF APOLLO

. . .]σ[. . .
. . . . . .]κιο[. . .
. . . .]πειτα[. . .
. . . . . .]πεσσυϑ[. . .
. . . . . .]γ[. . . . .]λ[. . . . .
. . . .]ω[. . .

(*This is sustained until the* FELLAHEEN *have finished setting
up the boxes. Then* GRENFELL *emerges from the rubbish tip
where he has fallen, now transformed into* APOLLO, *spitting out
the fragments.*)

GRENFELL/APOLLO

. . .]σ[. . .
. . . . . .]κιο[. . .
. . . .]πειτα[. . .
. . . . . .]πεσσυϑ[. . .
. . . . . .]γ[. . . . .]λ[. . . . .
. . . .]ω[. . .

I'm a god, Apollo, but I was tipped
on a rubbish tip inside this manuscript.
I've spent 2000 years asleep
on an Oxyrhynchus rubbish heap.
Till 1907 I had to wait
when Grenfell and Hunt came to excavate.
Covered in rubbish! But what's much worse is
being resurrected with scarcely half my verses.
Converted into dust and bookworm excreta
riddled lines with just a ghost of their metre.
All my speeches, all my precious words
mounting mounds of dust and millipede turds.
Ages under rubbish, sand, and desert heat
then be resurrected only half complete.
It's pathetic! Half the things I say
time or the desert mites have gnawn away.
But I'm Apollo and my role's to inspire us
so no more pauses for gaps in the papyrus.
And bit by bit we'll try to pick our way
slowly back through time and this lost satyr play.

Though I'm a deity and in everything divine
I still can get kerpertled about my kine.
You can't imagine how much it deeply grieves
even a god like me to lose his beeves.
My heart, though an immortal's, absolutely breaks
to think of all my loved ones turned into steaks.
Some light-fingered lout has filched my kine
that could well be kebabs washed down with wine.
What's that smell? I thought I could discern a
somewhat suspicious smell from a taverna.
It seemed for a moment that smell might mean a
meal of my moo-cows washed down with retsina.
It drives me out of my Apollonian mind
tracking down the cattle I just can't find
I've been all over Greece. So far! So far!
I'll bet my bulls are in some bugger's abattoir.
Who'd commit the sacrilege? Who'd dare? Who'd dare

spirit all my loved ones off into the air?
Man or immortal, it's hard to believe
someone had the cheek and gall to thieve
the cattle of the Sungod out of their byre.
I'm as furious as the Furies in the *Oresteia*.

Thessaly, Boeotia, the Doric (space . . . space . . . space)
then quickly to Kyllene, that's this place.
So, shepherd, farmer, charcoal burner,
layabout in the taverna
and, maybe in rustic parts like these,
descended from the Dryades,
the children of wild woodland creatures
with half human and half goat/horse features,
if *any* finds my cattle stolen from their lord,
Apollo, and returns them, he'll get a good reward.
There's backsheesh for the body who can track
down my stolen herd and bring them back.

HUNT

(*From inside tent*)

     Grenfell, Bernard? Are you *sure* you're all right?
     Enough work for today. You'll ruin your sight.
     It's too dark to decipher or delve in the sand.
     Shall I come out and give you a hand?

APOLLO

Hunt!

HUNT

(*From inside tent*)

     Coming! Coming! Just getting dressed.

APOLLO

Hunt out more fragments and find me the rest.
Hunt!

93

(*From inside tent*)

Coming!

APOLLO
Hunt for my kine!

HUNT/SILENUS
(*Emerging from tent*)

Evening, Apollo! Care for some wine?

I heard your proclamation, sir, and ran
or came as quickly as an old geezer can.
Us satyrs can help you. Our horse-like sniffers
'll soon track down your heisted bulls and heifers,
and maybe win, divine Apollo, Lord
whatever you're offering by way of reward.
If you could see your way, sir, to bestowing
backsheesh on the boys I'll get them going.
Summat beneficial. They'd have no quarrel
with gold, or liquid from a barrel,
but don't reckon too much to wreaths of laurel.
Summat boozable, Lord Apollo, please,
not leaf equivalents of OBEs.
The prospect of promotion to Sir Satyr
doesn't make my heart go pitter-patter.
You know us, all prancing, getting pissed
so forget your Olympian Honours List.
Summat gold or boozable? Are we both agreed?
Then I'll get the lads from the papyrus at top speed.

APOLLO
I must say I find you commendably keen.
I'll make you the foreman of my Fellaheen,
put you in charge of my 'Trackers', I mean.

94

(SILENUS *gazes towards the papyrus where we can see the waiting shadows of the* CHORUS OF SATYRS.
SILENUS *takes out a whistle.*)

SILENUS
I'll clog to life them loyal lads of mine.

(SILENUS *blows the whistle. The* SATYRS *do not enter.*)

APOLLO
You've lost your herd like me. I see no sign.

SILENUS
Well, 2000 years spent under the ground
might have taken the edge off my clogs' old sharp sound.
But you wait, your Godship, once I strut my stuff
my satyrs'll come like a shot, sure enough.

(*The* SATYRS *do not come.*)

APOLLO
Well? Where are they? Nothing to be seen.
They're as unreliable as the Fellaheen.

SILENUS
There's only one thing left to try
a few new-found fragments from the *Ichneutae*.

(*Lines projected above. Then projection of a line of waiting satyrs.*)

Look, there's the lads in all their old glory,
ready to come out and track down our story.

Behind that fragile vegetable matter's
a band of rumbustious bull-tracking satyrs
frozen by oblivion but all set
to answer any summons that they get.

95

So for you to help in tracking and make the play
   complete
I'll give you a few fragments to repeat:

ιϑ αγε δ] . . . . . . [
ποδα βα] . . . . . . [
απαπαπ] . . . . . . [
ω ω σε τοι] . . . . . . [

(*To* APOLLO)

Are they coming out? Are all my satyrs here?

APOLLO

No, they're stuck in the papyrus and don't want to
   appear.

(SILENUS *tries to work up the audience to chant the fragments
loud enough to bring the* SATYRS *out of the papyrus. He uses
some of the following lines if and when necessary.*)

SILENUS

Come on, come on. It'll be your fault,
now we've got going, if we grind to a halt.

APOLLO

I want the whole herd, every head, horn and tail.
So get your horse-snitches on to the trail.
You get me my cattle and what I'll give you's
gold bars as backsheesh you can barter for booze.
If you have any luck once you've got your lads out
and you find my herd for me, give me a shout.

(*Exit* APOLLO *through auditorium.*)

SILENUS

He gets that vicious when he's vexed,
so you'd better 'elp out and get lads from 'text.

96

Perhaps there's a doctor . . . some don from Queen's
who can tell the less educated what this means.

What's up? Been struck completely dumb
or is it the National Curriculum?

(*Greek chant now appears in readable Roman script.*)

Come on, you'll be the first to have a go
since about B C 450!

ιϑ αγε δ] . . . . . . [
ποδα βα] . . . . . . [
απαπαπ] . . . . . . [
ω ω σε τοι] . . . . . . [

(*When the chant is loud enough and sparks off its ancient
counterpart the crates of the Egypt Exploration Fund fly open,
each containing a* S A T Y R. *The crates form a grid which is the
dancing platform of the* S A T Y R S, *who wear clogs. The insides
of the crates are also painted as 'papyrus' and therefore double as
tracks of lost words and lost cattle.*)

After 2000 years, lads, look, there's your text.
It's up to you now to track what comes next.
And once you've tracked down each missing Greek
   word
then sniff out the trail of Apollo's lost herd.

CHORUS OF SATYRS
Group B
ιϑ αγε δ . . . . . . (bracket)
Group C
ποδα βα . . . . . . (bracket)
Group A
απαπαπ . . . . . . (bracket)
All
ω ω σε τοι . . . . . . (bracket)

97

Where cows tread . . . (track it . . . track it . . .)
Group C
near or far . . . (track it . . . track it . . .)
Group A
seek cow-clap . . . (track it . . . track it . . .)
All
however wee . . . (track it . . . track it . . .)

Group B
επιθι κλωπ . . . . . . (bracket)
Group C
υπονομα κ . . . . . . (bracket)
Group A
don't give up hope . . . (track it . . . track it . . .)
All
we'll get them back . . . (track it . . . track it . . .)

(*The* SATYRS *do their tracking dance.*)

Group B
Sniff, sniff
sniff at the track
we've gotta get t'god's cattle back.

Group C
Sniff, sniff
sniff with your snitch
sniff at the shit that'll make us all rich.

Group A
Sniff, sniff
sniff left and right
sniff every tincture of cattle-shite.

All
Sniff, sniff
sniff every turd
and get gold from t'god for tracking his herd.

Group B 4

If these are bulls' tracks,

Group B 5

their back legs go first

Group B 6

these bulls have had their bums reversed.

Groups A, C

Sniff, sniff
sniff without stopping
sniff every turd, sniff every dropping.

Group C 7

These tracks of t'god's herd,

Group C 8

if that's what we've found

Group C 9

look they're all of 'em the wrong way round.

Groups A, B

Sniff, sniff
sniff t'shit on t'ground
t'cattle-rustler's gotta be found.

Group A 1

Hey, look at this. It's stupid, daft.

Group A 2

Their back legs are forrad,

Group A 3

their front legs aft.

All

Sniff, sniff
sniff all the clues
that beckon to bullocks, backsheesh and *Booze*.

(*The* SATYRS *track again and suddenly there is an eerie sound which terrifies them. This is the sound of the newly-invented lyre. The* SATYRS' *clogs chatter with fear on the boards.*)

Group B

That sound!

Group C

  'orrible!

Group A

  Frightening!

Group B

         Scary!

Group C

           Spooky!

Group A 3

It's the prototype of the bazouki!

Group B

Don't care what it is.

Group C

  We're off back in the papyrus.

Group A

Stuff all this tracking.

SILENUS

You're pathetic. You're all made of jelly.
Every man/beast of you's a yeller belly.
You cowardly creeps, you dastardly dogs,
you're not fit to buckle or bull up my clogs.
Some shepherd's yell, some midget poodle's yap
and your clogs are all clarted with panicker's crap.
Unmanned, unhorsed by some moggy's meak miaou
made into cowards by one moo from a cow.
And if that sound had the merest hint of moo

it might well be t'god's herd these tracks have led to.
Scared of your own shadow, no spunk, no spine,
all talk and tupping, no true sons of mine.
Bragging and shagging, that's your style
but show you real action and you run a mile.
You say you'll stick by me, but come the crunch
you turn out such a yeller-bellied bunch.

But Silenus in his day, he never fled.
He faced all dangers with no shred of dread.
Silenus the satyr, never short of spunk
braved every battle, never did a bunk.
He was a warrior, valorous, not weak
not thrown in a panic by a mere squawk or squeak.
When fierce battle raged I never quit –
there I was always in the thick of it.
A hero with honour from many a campaign,
the honour your cowardice will now stain.
Think of an old soldier having to see
his own battalion turn tail and flee,
the ones he brags about as his 'brave boys'
ready to desert the field because of a mere noise,
some squawk, some squeak, some tu-whit-tu-whoo.
A fieldmouse's fart's enough to scare you.
Fabled as I am for many a noble feat
it breaks this soldier's heart to see you in retreat.
You'd piss off if you heard a parrot sneeze.

CHORUS OF SATYRS
A 1

Come here,

A 2

.then,

you hero,

   Group A

      and play Hercules.

   All

Yer,

   B 4

    come here yourself, if you have no fear.

   B 5

If you are so brave,

   B 6

    then, you should have been here.

   C 7

If you brave dangers,

   C 8

    brave this one now.

   C 9

Then tell us we're only scared of some cow.

   All

Ay,

   A 1

    show us this famous courage of yours.

   A 2

See how you feel

   A 3

    when the grim monster roars.

   All

It's a sound like nowt ever 'eard before.
It struck terror in us right down to the core.

SILENUS

I am the hunter and you are the pack

and the hunter, when tracking, leads from the back.
But if an old soldier has to instil
courage in cowards, then instil I will.
I'll lead the rabble, if you so choose
and pump up your courage with hunter's halloos.
When a fierce commander stands at their head
even base cowards forget to feel dread.
When cowards are led by commanders like me
they see my example, stand fast, and don't flee.

(SILENUS *puffs out his chest, stands erect, and leads the*
SATYRS *in a dance. The dance reaches a crescendo, then is cut
off by the sound of the newly-invented lyre. This time* SILENUS
hears it too.)

I'll let you do the tracking. I'm getting too old.

(*Exit* SILENUS.)

CHORUS OF SATYRS
But he'll be back later for his share of the gold.

(*The sound of the lyre.*
The SATYRS *are now determined to find the source of the noise,
a sound never heard before on the face of the earth.*
They start to dance out the one responsible for the noise.)

Group B
Out!
Or we'll clog out such clatters
you'll be sorry you ever scared us poor satyrs.

Group C
Out!
You can't get away
you're stuck same as us in Sophocles' play.

103

Group A

Out! Out!
Come on YOU
the papyrus says 'enter' but not enter WHO.

All

Out!
Your first words are here
you say 'bestial creatures' when you appear.

(SATYRS *begin to drop out of the dance, exhausted. Three of them create a 'Theatre of Dionysus' out of the Egypt Exploration Fund crates in front of the papyrus with some boxes on their sides to allow* SATYRS *inside to appear to be supporting the stage as they do in the Theatre of Dionysus in Athens.*)

B 5

We're that knackered from dancing.
B 4

Give us a break

B 6

and please make an entrance,
All

for Sophocles' sake.

3 SATYRS

(*From under stage*)

Satyr 1

Up there tragic heroes cry WOE!
Satyr 2

WOE!

Satyr 3

WOE!

Satyr 2

while us poor bloody satyrs are groaning below!

104

C 7

They've set up the stage

C 8

       as it might have been

C 9

when you had your first chance of playing the scene.

A 1

We've checked the papyrus.

A 2

         Your part's more intact

A 3

than most of the other parts

Group A

       that we've tracked.

All

We've done all the work. You don't have to track it
or get bamboozled by bracket, bracket, BRACKET!

KYLLENE

(*Entering through the papyrus*)

    Bestial creatures! Cease your coarse racket!
Bestial creatures! Wherefore have you brought
to this secluded spot your uproar foul?
What novel sports are these? They are not they
wherewith of old you made your master glad
who, clad in his fawnskin and with thyrsus high,
was wont to chant of yore the holy hymns
with, for escort, nymphs and youthful throngs.

    Now I know not what possesseth you
nor what crazed folly spinneth you awry . . .
I heard like hunters' halloos from deep within
a cry when keen trackers close upon their prey

105

and hap upon the beast deep in its lair.
And then such harsh words as thief assailed mine ears.
Your fragments of furore reached me down there
and then such an utter cacophony commenced
I feared that you would do my person harm.

CHORUS OF SATYRS
(Joining in the elevated 'tragic' tone)

A 1
Stay thine anger,
A 2
nymph of the deep zone,
A 3
we are no bringers of disruptive strife.

All
Nay,
B 4
all that we humbly wish is that you disclose
the meaning
B 5
of that hidden sound we heard.

KYLLENE
That is a better way to learn what you desire
than by alarming 'ere a poor defenceless nymph.
Quarrelling is most distressing to my soul.
Now I implore proceed and make your plea.

CHORUS OF SATYRS
B 6
Ruler of this region,
C 7
Kyllene,
C 8
Queen,

106

our purpose later will we you explain.

A 1

But this voice we heard,

A 2

    what is it, pray?

A 3

It frayed our nerves

B 4

    and set our teeth on edge.

B 5

Who is it that bringeth the gooselumps on our flesh?

B 6

What is it raiseth the spine hairs on our backs?

KYLLENE

I must advise you ere I do commence,
should you disclose what I to you disclose,
there will be severest suffering in store.

Zeus hither hied where Maia doth abide,
all unbeknownst to Hera, hither hied
and made the fair one his clandestine bride.

In the cave the nymph brought forth a son
the which, because his mother Maia
doth languish in a fever, nurse I in these arms.
But the babe doth burgeon greatly day by day.
'Tis a great wonder to me and a fright.
Born six days ago and yet hath manhood reached.
He blossometh upwards daily without a pause.
Such is the babe whose nurture have I here.
We conceal him for his mighty father's sake.

As for the sound which caused you such a fright
bursting forth from some source still concealed
it came from something turned the wrong way up.
The babe I nurse devised it in a day

107

from a dead creature as a source of joy.
He plays this strange device both night and day.

3 SATYRS

(*From under the stage*)

I hope that's the end. My back's giving way.

CHORUS OF SATYRS
All

Ay,

B 5

bugger the whatsit,

B 4

and the miraculous boy

B 6

wanking about with the dead creature toy.

C 9

Excuse me, but how can summat dead

C 8

sing?

C 7

How come a voice came from a dead thing?

A 1

Dead but vocal.

A 2

A corpse that can carol?

A 3

Somebody's snout's been into the barrel.

B 4

A stiff and it warbles.

All
How come?

B 5, 6

Ay, how come?

KYLLENE

Dead it has a voice. Alive it was dumb.

108

CHORUS OF SATYRS
All

Give us a clue.

C 9
Is it bent,
C 8
fat,
C 7
short,
All
or what?

KYLLENE

'Tis spotted and shaped somewhat like a pot.

CHORUS OF SATYRS
A 2

A leopard,

All
of course,

A 1, 3
or some sort of cat.

KYLLENE

No, sorry. It's nothing at all like that.

CHORUS OF SATYRS
B 4

Not a crab,

B 5
not a lobster,
B 6
not a crustacean . . .

All

Then it's gotta be

Group B
the bug part of creation.

                              All
       A beetle!
                              C 9
              The Etna horned scarab,
                              All
                                        mayhap?

                         SATYR 2
(*From under the stage*)

       Solve her damned riddle and cut all the crap!

                    CHORUS OF SATYRS
                              All
       Madam,
                              A 3
              what bit of it makes that horrible din?
                              A 1
       Is that nasty noise from outside or in?

                         KYLLENE
       From what you might call the creature's crust.

                         SATYRS
(*From under the stage*)

       Solve t'bloody riddle. My head's going to bust.

                    CHORUS OF SATYRS
                              All
       If we may be so presumptuous as to inquire . . .

                         KYLLENE
       The beast's called a tortoise. The invention . . . the lyre!

(KYLLENE *gestures to the papyrus where the projection of the
baby* HERMES *with the lyre appears. The lyre sounds again.
The* SATYRS *listen and try to imitate its pitch.*)

CHORUS OF SATYRS

Group B

It could be a goat
to judge from its note

All

BUT!

Group A

It could be a duck's
the guts that he plucks

All

BUT!

Group C

It could be a cat
a cat sounds like that

All

BUT!

Group B

It could be a hound's
hounds make them sounds

All

BUT!

Bet it's bullock gut!

Group B

Summat's been flayed
for this sweet serenade

B 4

It's not just the tortoise's hollow shell

B 6

there's some other creature in there as well.

III

Summat's been flayed
for this sweet serenade.

                    C 7
It isn't just a tortoise is it though?
                    C 9
There's some other sound in it.
                    Group C
                                        Some sort of low!

                    Group A
Summat's been flayed
for this sweet serenade.

                    A 1
Some other sound keeps coming through.
                    A 2
It's more than a tortoise.
                    A 3
                        It's got like a
                    All
                                        moo!

It could be a goat
to judge from its note.
It could be a duck's
the guts that he plucks.
It could be a cat
a cat sounds like that
sweet serenade.

And the question is
to this kid that's the whizz
where did you get that gut?

Them leather thongs
he twangs into songs

to comfort, or, maybe, carouse,
we don't have to go through
the whole bloody zoo
they come from Apollo's nicked cows.

(KYLLENE *is tipped off the stage, losing her pediment. Four* SATYRS *try to lift it and can't.* KYLLENE *bends and lifts it up on to her head again with effortless Olympic lift.* KYLLENE *tries to exit and finds her way blocked each time by a lascivious* SATYR. *Finally* KYLLENE *escapes to the tent and closes the flap.*)

CHORUS OF SATYRS
All
It's no use to you, it's marble that minge.
Let's get t'gold from t'god and go on a binge.

Group B
Booze! Booze!
We've tracked down the clues
now we want our backsheesh and . . . αγ εια νυ . . .
   BRACKET!

Group C
Booze! Booze!
We've tracked down the clues
now we want . . . . . . ω Λοξια δε . . . BRACKET!

Group A
Booze! Booze!
We've tracked down the . . . των βοων . . . BRACKET!

All
Booze! Booze! Booze! Booze! (etc.)

(*Light fades to blackout. 'Booze!' continues.*
*The '*BRACKET*' takes out the lights and in the dark we hear the* 'Booze!' *repeated softer and softer until it sounds like lowing*

cattle. Enter A P O L L O *down centre gangway, bearing light*.)

APOLLO
Those are my loved ones. I know by their moos.

(A P O L L O *'s 'spot' focuses on each* S A T Y R *in turn, who speaks*.)

Where are my loved ones? Give them to me
then I'll give you the gold and set you all free.

CHORUS OF SATYRS
B 5
Them lovely moo-cows you mooned over, squire,
all that's left of the lot is that little lad's lyre.

C 9
The strings of that thing came from your herd's guts
and them were the horns that waved once on their nuts.

A 3
And look at that, squire, that membrane of hide.
Bet it came off a flayed bullock's backside.

B 4
Of all your prize bullocks there's nowt left to show
B 6
but a dribbling baby with homemade banjo.

C 8
Sorry to tell you but
C 7
that little lad
's squeezed all your steers into t'prototype Strad.

A 1
We've tracked 'em the length and breadth of the land
A 2
and now all they're fit for's to play in a band.

114

All

Sorry to inform you, sir, this lyre
's all you've got left of the bulls from your byre.

APOLLO

He'll have to be quizzed this whizz-kid you've tracked
and you'll be rewarded, as per our pact.
This bovver babe, this bovicidal maniac.
I'll beat him black and blue to get my bulls back.
Fetch him out! Fetch him out! He'll feel my fist
this infant instrumentalist!

(SATYRS *start clogging*)

Fetch him out! I'll do him in
I'll make a drum from the little sod's skin.

Fetch him out! I'll have the lad flayed
for flaying my cattle for his serenade.

Fetch him out! Fetch him out! He'll feel my fist
this infant instrumentalist.

(*The* SATYRS *clog to a crescendo.
The projection of the baby* HERMES *with lyre disappears,
replaced by a white spot which moves to the opening in the
papyrus. A lyre emerges in a hand, baby-height, through the gap
in the papyrus. As the clogging reaches a climax,* HERMES
enters through the papyrus and APOLLO *and the* SATYRS *back
away.*)

APOLLO

Hermes, whizz-kid, son of Zeus and Maia
you're the thief who stole my herd from its byre,
and dehorned and degutted they went into your lyre.

HERMES

How can you say that? Herd? Herd?

I'm only five days old. I've never heard the word.
Never heard of 'herd'. No, sorry, pet,
herd isn't in my lexicon yet.
I'm still trying to learn the alphabet.
Listen to my lyre. This is my invention.
Listen to its magic. Pay attention!

(HERMES *plays on the lyre so melodiously that* APOLLO *and the* SATYRS *are charmed.* APOLLO *is sufficiently intrigued to want the lyre in exchange for his cattle.*)

APOLLO

Fellow immortal, son of Zeus and Maia,
I beg you to teach me the art of the lyre.
This was all fated. I feel it was meant
for my sole use this soothing instrument.

(APOLLO *tries to snatch the lyre from* HERMES.)

HERMES

Gerroff my lyre. I made it. It's mine!

APOLLO

But I'm older than you, and a lot more divine.
Give me your gadget. Be a good boy.
I could give class to your trivial toy.

HERMES

But it's boring for a baby in t'cradle all day.
I'd go proper potty with no lyre to play.
She wouldn't even give me a rattle
so I made this thing out of your cattle.

APOLLO

Let me have your gadget, or you'll get a good slap.
That papyrus he's wearing is full of warm crap.

(HERMES *sobs.*)

116

There, there, little fellow! But you're scarcely fit
to give lyre recitals with pants full of shit.
You're frankly disgusting. I think that the lyre
requires a performer in more formal attire.
Change your crappy papyrus while I serenade
these lowly satyrs with the lyre that you made.

HERMES

How will I be a grown-up god like you
and live on Olympus with pants full of poo?

(*Exit* HERMES.)

APOLLO

At last! At last! Well, here goes.

(APOLLO *plays a few arpeggios*.)

The first Apollonian arpeggios!

Simply by plucking these magical strings
I can raise my soul and man's to higher things.
Deserts, a papyrus torn to tatters,
theft, a trail of turds, and sniffing satyrs.
From that unpromising, unlikely start
from barrenness and shit we have brought ART!

This mottled tortoise, this creeping thing
joined to my cattle makes dumb nature sing.
Debeeved, bereaved, but now I can rejoice
that was dead and dumb now has a voice.
I rather think the tortoise population
will be proud to make music for higher creation,
proud to be the sole purveyor/supplier
of the principal part of Apollo's own lyre.

The gods decreed a fixed scale in creation
from the Olympian, like me, to the crustacean,

117

and almost at the bottom of the scale,
even below your sort with hoof and tail,
and tail-bearers with no part human, come
creatures like this tortoise, who are dumb.
The scale of creation like a scale with notes
runs the whole gamut from gods to goats,
and distinctly closer to the latter,
low on the scale of being, comes the satyr.

CHORUS OF SATYRS
Group B
It's very sad, the tortoise had to die,
as part goat or horse, I part identify.

Group C
When Nature gets made use of for Man's needs
my heart, at least the goat part of it, bleeds.

Group A
But when I hear the lyre, all the rest,
the two-thirds human part, 's impressed.

Group B
We're always in things from the very start,
the creation of fire, the lyre, wine and art.

Group C
We're envoys of Nature who give their consent
to surrender the substance they use to invent.

Group A
Woodlands for barbecues, crushed grapes for wine
but where will a satyr start drawing the line?

APOLLO
When Dionysus started giving wine away
the horse part of you satyrs never said neigh.
Soon you'll be free to drink till you fall,

the freedom, it seems, you want most of all.
But first you satyrs, and you people out there,
listen to my lyre's world première.

(APOLLO *gives the world's first lyre recital. The* SATYRS *are
enraptured by the melody, so much so that when* APOLLO *has
finished his recital the* SATYRS *all rush forward and crowd
round* APOLLO, *reaching up towards the lyre.*)

CHORUS OF SATYRS
All
Oh, it's wonderful. Let us have a go!

APOLLO
No! No! No! No! No!

My advice is stick to being satyrs
and don't go meddling in musical matters.
You don't need lyres. You're natural celebrators
stuck between animal and human status.
You need no consolations of high art.
Your human pain's cancelled by your horse/goat part.
What use are lyres to you? Your satyr stamp and strut
has no need of these seven strings of gut.
You're satyrs, satyrs. Your sort need no lyres
while your goat parts tether you to brute desires.

Your capers and your clogs' staccato clatter's
exactly the racket expected of satyrs.
My lyre will create that sort of élite
that will never get caught out tapping its feet
or think for a second that twanging these strings
gives licence for furtive fandangoes and flings.
Apollo's new public won't prance, they'll keep
so still when they listen you'll think them asleep.
Your 'music', and I put that firmly in quotes,
is suitable only for brutish men/goats.
The point of my music is to put a stop
to your type of prancing and clippety-clop.

119

This is now my lyre and I define
its music as half-human, half-divine,
and satyrs, half-beasts, must never aspire
to mastering my, and I mean *my*, lyre.

(*The* SATYRS *are a devastated bunch.*)

But I have to grant that you did the bit
I couldn't descend to sniffing the shit.
Yes I have to concede that you sniffed out the track
and got me what's left of my cattle back.
You kept your promise. My cattle got tracked.
You'll get what I promised as per our pact.
There's gold for you all, though no doubt you'll fritter
the whole bloody lot on barrels of bitter.
Gold and freedom. You're free, if you stay
where you belong, in the crude Satyr Play.

(APOLLO *plays his lyre again, while* KYLLENE *emerges from
the tent and, like some Lady Mayoress, presents the* SATYRS
*with large bars of gold, in fact ghetto-blasters wrapped in gold
foil.
They take their gifts to the Oxyrhynchus rubbish mounds and sit
gazing at their reflections in the gold foil, aware for the first time
of the division between their animal and human selves.
As they stare into their gold bars* APOLLO *begins his exit but
turns to address the audience in a way that assumes they are all
Apollonian.*)

APOLLO
I forsee in ages yet to unfold
my statue in temples of marble and gold.
Palaces of culture with gold statues of me
will preside over music and poetry.
Where I'm on the pediment, where I preside,
no creatures with tails will set clog inside.
They tracked down my lyre and now that I've thanked 'em
their clogs aren't allowed in my musical sanctum.

That holy of holies was never intended
for creatures with dicks so grossly distended.
Any one item, cock, clog or tail
puts them beyond the Apollonian pale.
When the lyre casts its spell men won't remember
the satyr with clogs and disgusting great member.
In my world of music I set the tone
in a thoroughly clogless desatyrized zone.
While I am the one with the lyre and the wreath
satyrs will always be pushed underneath.

I prophesy that they'll track through the ages
and end up where you saw them, underneath stages.
Their clogs will condemn them to lowly positions
and the words they'll track down will all be petitions.

To those whose snouts were made to sniff turds
I bequeath Greek petitions and four-letter words,
and those who pass by them on the way to my shrine
will shy away sharp from their beggarly whine.
Numbed by the cold and numbed by strong drink
the refugee satyrs will mistakenly think
if they flock near the lyre Apollonians might,
their hearts opened by music, attend to their plight.
I prophesy cloggies are condemned to speak
only the hopeless petitioners' Greek.
μη μεταναστης . . . 'don't make me a stray'
cry the vagrants evicted out of their play.
μη μεταναστης . . . they'll find every street
strewn with petitions like that to repeat.
I'll keep the poetry and cloggies like those
will have to exist on petitioners' prose.

(APOLLO *gets handfuls of papyri from the 'petitions' crate and
scatters them about. He keeps those from the 'poetry and plays'.)*

In order to win this lyre that I'm strumming
I had to go in for some serious slumming.

Now the lyre's been invented and in my god's grip
the papyrus goes back on the rubbish tip.
I don't think I ever want to leave clues
that music's supremo had shit on his shoes.
There'll be in the future an unbridgeable split
between the spirit of music and mere mention of shit.
No clues should remain I had any connections
with clog-footed satyrs with gruesome erections.
If it's ever deciphered the papyrus there proves
Apollo consorted with creatures with hooves.
Henceforward Apollo will only guest-star
in a thoroughly satyrless repertoire.

I could destroy it myself. It's more of a wheeze
if they do the dirty on Sophocles.

Now I'll play my lyre and make rise
Apollonian temples in front of your eyes.

(APOLLO *plays his 'tune' again, and his 'tune' contains in it the
string orchestras of the future. On the papyrus appear projections
of various opera houses and theatres, say, Vienna Staatsoper,
Munich Met, New York, and ending with Covent Garden, Royal
Royal Festival Hall, and Royal National Theatre.*)

O Apollonian pile. My prophetic wits
tell me that this tune will be one of my hits.
And tell me that this is the tune I'll be playing
when their brother Marsyas suffers his flaying.

I feel the future put out a call
for me and my lyre to the Festival Hall.

(*Exit* APOLLO *playing his 'tune', fading fainter and fainter.
The* SATYRS *begin opening their gold-wrapped gifts. Beneath
the gold foil are today's newspapers,* The Times, Financial
Times, Guardian, Independent, *all the papers. They examine
the wrappings as novelties. New rubbish tips are created.*)

B 4

Who wants some stupid tortoise to strum?

C 7

He can stick his bloody banjo up his bum.

A 1

Once it gains a foothold in our habitat
with its plinkety-plonk, well, that'll be that.

B 5

It'll be in t'woods, in t'hills, in t'air –

C 8

even in t'toilet and that's everywhere.

A 2

There'll be no stretch of sky, no bit of ground
that won't in the end be full of its sound.

B 6

You watch what'll happen. It'll force birds
out of business, as songsters, you mark my words.

C 9

Ay, birdsong's passé. The lyre'll usurp
the song of the skylark, the chaffinch's chirp.

A 3

The beginning of the end. You wait and see,
there'll be plinkety-plonk behind every damn tree.

(*By this time the* SATYRS *have slowly unwrapped the gold foil
and the layers of newspapers to reveal the ghetto-blasters, which
stand on the mounds before them. The* SATYRS *don't
understand their function. Suddenly from all the ghetto-blasters
at once comes the terrifying scream of Marsyas with a*

sound like the tuning up of a large string section of an orchestra, the descendents of the lyre tuning up for the concerts of the future such as those in the Royal Festival Hall. The SATYRS' *clogs chatter on the boards, then they flee.* SILENUS *silences the ghetto-blasters*.)

SILENUS

That's Marsyas screaming! They ripped off his skin
and all he ever wanted was to join in.
Marsyas suffered his terrible flaying
for a bit of innocent *aulos* playing.

The *aulos*, Athene's flute. She flung it away
so why shouldn't Marsyas pick it up and play?
A few blows and the goddess gave the flute
she'd just invented the elegant boot.
She flung the thing aside. Do you know why?
Well, think of the *aulos*. Ever had a try?
You puff your cheeks out, like this, when you play
and she didn't like her face to look that way.
She thought it unattractive. Well, its true
her cheeks looked like balloons when she blew.
And who should find the flung flute in the grass
but my brother satyr, Marsyas?
Questions of cosmetics scarcely matter
to one who has the ugly mug of a satyr.
It's not for good looks that us satyrs are noted
so Marsyas blew and let his cheeks get bloated.
He took himself off to a quiet bit of wood
and girned and puffed and grunted and got good.
That peeved Apollo. He'd crossed the bounds.
Half-brutes aren't allowed to make beautiful sounds.
And can't you just hear those Muses say:
'Who gave a common satyr licence to play?'
Music's an inner circle meant to exclude
from active participation a beast so crude.
'How can he be a virtuoso on the flute?
Look at the hooves on him. He's half a brute!'

124

His one and only flaw was to show that flutes
sound just as beautiful when breathed into by brutes.
It confounds their categories of high and low
when your Caliban outplays your Prospero.
If Marsyas had touched it and said 'ooo'
the way us satyrs are supposed to do,
but he went and picked it up and blew the flute
and that was trespassing for the man/brute.

For them it would have been quite enough
to have given it one abortive puff,
a buffoonish ballooning of the brutish cheeks
producing a few and inexpert squeaks.
That would have amused them and been OK
but Marsyas, man/animal, learned to play.
To have watched him smell it, test it with his teeth
or use it like the pygmies as a penis sheath,
all allowable, all tolerated fun,
but your Apollonian goes for his gun
when it suddenly dawns on him that the swine
the pearl is cast before by one divine
knows it's a pearl, and not some novel food
and aspires beyond dumb swinetude.
When he enters the culture the 'pearl' represents
they reach for their skin-removing instruments.

They set up a contest, rigged from the start,
to determine the future of 'high' and 'low' art.
They had it all fixed that Apollo should win
and he ordered my brother to be flayed of his skin.
And the Phrygian skinner with his flaying blade
saw Apollo's pointing pinkie and obeyed.
While Marsyas suffered his terrible flaying
Apollo looked on with his 'doodah' playing.
While the Phrygian flenser slices and flays
Apollo plucks out a glib Polonaise.
And the skinners applauded Apollo's reprise
as my brother's flayed nipples flapped on to his knees.

The last thing Marsyas saw was his own skin
like a garment at his feet with no one in.

Wherever the losers and the tortured scream
the lyres will be playing the Marsyas theme.
You'll hear the lyres playing behind locked doors
where men flay their fellows for some abstract cause.
The kithara cadenza, the Muse's mezzo trill
cover the skinning and the screaming still.
Wherever in the world there is torture and pain
the powerful are playing the Marsyas refrain.
In every dark dungeon where blood has flowed
the lyre accompanies the Marsyas Ode.

Wherever the racked and the anguished cry
there's always a lyre-player standing by.
Some virtuoso of Apollo's ur-violin
plays for the skinners as they skin.

(SILENUS *drinks from his wineskin as if to blot out the
memory of Marsyas*.)

So I don't make waves. I don't rock the boat.
I add up the plusses of being man/goat.
Unlike my poor flayed brother, Marsyas
I've never yearned to move out of my class.
In short, I suppose, I'm not really averse
to being a satyr. I could do a lot worse.
I just have to find the best way to exist
and I've found, to be frank, I exist best pissed.

(SILENUS *drinks. His wineskin has run out. He seeks in the
rubbish tips for a cider bottle. He drinks from that*.)

Pathetic! What a pathetic decline
for one who witnessed the first pressing of wine.
And when the first vintage was picked from the vine
who watched it ferment, who supped the first wine?

Us! Us us us.
I was there at the birth of wine and of fire
both more use here than that bleeding lyre.

(*Drinks*)

Oblivion's not what we once were about.
We drank to praise life, not blot it all out.
One who led the Trackers of Oxyrhynchus,
a Dionysian, down here with meths-drinkers!
But the young ones, they're bitter. They're not like me,
they deface and destroy all papyri they see.
They gash 'em, graffiti 'em, ay, and they'd spray
FUCK, PISS and SHIT all over our play
if I weren't here watching, keeping my eye
on what scraps are left of our *Ichneutae*.

(*We hear* 3 SATYR/HOOLIGANS *chanting off. They enter with already defaced pieces of papyri, ripped and graffitied. They carry aerosols. They deface the papyrus on the dancing floor with obscenities and the name of Marsyas.*)

SATYR/HOOLIGANS
Satyr 1

Fuck! Fuck!
Who gives a fuck?
Who wants a place in papyrus or book.

Satyr 2

Fuck! Fuck!
Fuck being part
of all that poncy Apollonian art.

Satyr 3

Fuck! Fuck!
Fuck the papyrus!
A piss-up's all we need to inspire us.

All

Fuck! Fuck!
Fuck the god's lyre
this is the Harp that satyrs require.

(*They open Harp lager cans and spray* SILENUS *with the
exploding froth. This wakes him from his drunken snooze.*)

SILENUS
(*Seeing them now threaten the hanging papyrus*)

You've had your fun there. Don't harm that bit!
Keep that intact, or we're all in the shit.
Don't harm the papyrus. Don't blur one iota
or we'll never again have a home we can go to.
Don't harm the papyrus. It gave us our start.
It gave us our one chance of starring in art.
Marsyas wouldn't want revenge of that sort
so don't count on his ghost to give you support.
Don't blur one iota. Every scrap matters
if we're ever to get our rights back as satyrs.
Don't harm the papyrus. That's where we come from.

SATYR/HOOLIGANS
Fuck off, you fucking old Uncle Tom!

Satyr 1
Your gold-nosing, god-arse-licking ways
betraying your brothers by tracking down plays.
Satyr 2
Your yes sir, no sir, track your cow, sir's
the reason we're stuck here wearing trousers.
Satyr 3
And you, you've only got Apollo to thank
Satyr 2
You're here with blue balls
Satyr 1
                    on the freezin' South Bank.

Satyr 3
First he's all friendly, the godly gladhand,
next there's a notice: ALL SATYRS BANNED.
Satyr 1
Then come the brackets, the new double locks
and NO ADMISSION TO SATYRS WITH COCKS.
Satyr 2
You, you gormless grovelling sod
being so servile to that sodding god
got us stuck here in Great bloody Britain
where nowt about satyrs'll ever get written.
Satyr 3
Your track-sniffing satyrs are now sniffing glue
and you want to preserve this thing as a clue.
Satyr 1
A clue to what then?
Satyrs 1, 2 and 3
                    Don't make us laugh!
Satyr 1
A sort of satyr Ceno-
Satyr 2
                    fucking-
Satyr 3
                              taph
Satyr 1
with Apollonians with long faces laying
wreaths to commemorate
Satyrs 1, 2 and 3
                    Marsyas' flaying.

SILENUS
Don't you dare take my brother's name in vain.
What do you lads know of his hopes or his pain.
Don't tell me. I was there. I was there.
I heard his sickening screams rend the air.
The sound of the skin as it started to tear.
When it was over at Apollo's command
the hide was defrizzed and curried and tanned.

129

The first thing they cut off and flung to the dogs
was his cock, the next thing his clogs.
They kept a bull mastiff as defatter/demeater
and they tanned the hide in the mastiff's excreta.
My brother's flayed skin was flung in a pit
with a brew-up of boiling water and shit.
Marsyas' membrane massaged with greases
until it was free of all wrinkles and creases,
defrizzed to smoothness, scoured of its scud
and praise-hymns penned on it in my brother's blood.
A surface so smooth it took penman's letters
and paeans composed in praise of his 'betters'.
Send the scholars to me. I'll tell 'em. I'll tell 'em
the violence and filth that made the first vellum.

So don't harm the papyrus. It's one vital clue
the lyre depended on such lads as you.
It's taken years, and such trouble, to reconstruct
so don't you destroy it . . .

SATYR/HOOLIGANS
Go and get fucked!

SILENUS
That papyrus I tell you is our only chance
of getting our clogs back into the dance.

SATYR/HOOLIGANS
Satyr 1
We don't dance no more to let off our steam.
How can you dance to the Marsyas scream?

Satyr 2
They made us keep hooves on so they could track
wherever we are with t'clogs' clackety-clack.

Satyr 3
These hooves we once danced with and strutted our stuff

130

come in really handy when the going gets rough.

Satyr 1
Them hooves that we pranced in in that shit play
do very nicely for

G!
Satyr 3
B!
Satyr 2
H!
Satyrs 1, 2 and 3
OK?

(*They boot* SILENUS *in the face and balls.*)

Satyr 1
O very handy your satyr hoof/clog
Satyr 2
for one in the phallus!
Satyr 3
One in the physog!

Satyr 1
They might have been fine for that old-fashioned strut
but they're brilliant for booting a bloke in the gut.

(*They boot* SILENUS *again in face and balls.
The* SATYR/HOOLIGANS *flee. We hear their clogs run down
streets and on to the South Bank outside. The clogs fade and in
its place we hear the sound of shuffling clogs, soft at first.*)

SILENUS
(*Recovering*)

They don't see it, do they, silly young fools
how divine Apollo divides us and rules.

(SILENUS *notices that the piece of papyrus graffitied with the name 'Marsias' is spelt wrongly*)

> But look in the end it's that that makes you cry.
> They've spelt my brother's name with an I.

(SILENUS *corrects the I to a Y with his 'blood'*)

> Marsyas would have organized schools
> to teach better spelling to these bloody fools.
> With face and body bloodied do I qualify
> to move up from 'low' art into the 'high'?

(*Looks at stage*)

> We've all served our time with that weight on our heads
> but no satyr ever trod where tragedy treads.
> Gods, heroes and kings are all who walk there,
> high and low divided just by a stair.
> This is my big chance. But I don't dare.
> A lifetime's conditioning makes me refrain
> from attempting, a satyr, the high tragic strain.
> A lifetime's conditioning makes me afraid
> that to step a rung higher will get misself flayed.
> And I'd never know the right words to speak
> after 2000 years I've forgotten my Greek.
>
> But you can help out. Perhaps, perhaps
> you could oblige me by pronouncing these scraps.
> It's not much to ask you, is it, to spare
> an old entertainer a few lungfuls of air?
> Just enough to get me set off on the track
> where the lads are all waiting. I want to go back.

(*The shuffling clogs and the petitioners' phrases get louder and we again see the projection of the satyrs on the papyrus.*)

> Look, there's the lads in all their old glory

just waiting for t'piss-up to round off the story.

By these sacred fragments of Sophocles
don't make me homeless, I beg of you, please!
Look at the papyrus and read me what's written
and give me a home here in Great Britain
or failing that just chant it and release
me and the lads back to Ancient Greece.

(*Silence from the audience who can't read papyri. Sound of louder petitions from behind the papyrus.*)

All I'm asking, begging's for you to recite
a few words of Greek to release me tonight
of the sun and the clear sky that shone on our play
when we last did it in Sophocles' day.

(*Silence from the audience who can't read papyri. Sound of petitions from behind the papyrus.*)

Is there a doctor . . . some don from Queen's
who can tell the rest of us what all this means?

(*Silence from audience.
Sound of petitions from behind the papyrus.*)

Look, there's the lads in all their old glory
just waiting for t'piss-up to round off the story.

I know that it's missing the end of the *Trackers*
but it's bound to have ended with worshipping
   Bacchus,
a piss-up with the boys the papyrologists missed,
the lines at the end say 'Now let's get pissed'.

Don't I deserve a little reward?
I'm not even asking you to applaud.
Just help me get away from this bloody cold river
that doesn't half make a poor satyr shiver.

(*Finds overcoat and cap in rubbish tip.*
The petitions grow louder behind the papyrus and in the
auditorium.)

> I get it! No one reads Greek. Neither do I
> so it's not much bloody use, the *Ichneutae*.

(*Petitions get louder and louder.*)

> And if I'm stuck here in this freezing void
> that papyrus up there can be better employed.

(SILENUS *pulls down the papyrus, revealing the* SATYRS,
now dressed like the South Bank homeless but with their satyr
skins, cocks, and tails visible in the plastic bags they carry.
The SATYRS *move forward, shuffling towards the rubbish*
heaps, saying the petition Greek and picking over the
newspapers, the torn text of The Trackers of Oxyrhynchus,
National Theatre posters for Trackers *etc.*
All they can say is the phrase μη μεταναστης *from the*
Oxyrhynchus petition which they say to the audience in various
ways, always disappointed by the non-response.)

(*Pulling the papyrus into a heap.*)

> I wouldn't bother, boys, if I were you.
> Them fucking petitions'll never get through.
> You can stand there and petition all week
> and get bugger all. No one knows Greek.

(*Shredding the papyrus*)

> Here, lads, some bedding. Make a thick layer
> of Sophocles against this freezing night air.

(*The* SATYRS *shred the papyrus and make shelters from the*
Egypt Exploration Fund crates adjoining the crates that made the
stage of the Theatre of Dionysus.

Behind them as they build fade up projections of NT and RFH.
The PALE BOY clutches a satyr costume to himself and stares
out. SILENUS distributes small bits of papyrus.)

Here take this little bit
it'll come in handy after a shit.

Stuff your lugs with this to keep out the sound
of music and drama when you kip on the ground.

With your ear on the concrete what you can hear
is Ligeti in one lug and in t'other *King Lear*
competing with the pelting 'of the pitiless storm'
up there in the RNT where it's nice and warm.

Here, make earplugs of this so no Birtwistle number
will rudely break into your South Bank slumber.

And here it's ποδα βα and απαπαπ
take it and use it after a crap.

He was sensitive, a poet, was Sophocles,
he wouldn't have wanted his satyrs to freeze.
But he was a poet and he'd probably follow,
when it came to the crunch, the laws of Apollo.
Well, I'll be his spokesman and say I don't mind
if you use my papyrus to wipe your behind.
I am happy that my long-lost Satyr Play's
divided up into Andrex and dossers' duvets.

(The SATYRS *build their crate city on the spot where the Theatre
of Dionysus was. They make bedding of papyrus and settle down
for the night.* SILENUS *moves toward the* PALE BOY, *who is
staring out, clutching a satyr costume. We hear music from the
Royal Festival Hall, Apollo's 'tune'. The* PALE BOY *gags on
fragments of the word 'Apollo'. The* SATYRS *are settling down
to sleep, in their papyrus duvets.*
SILENUS *tenderly wraps the* PALE BOY *in his 'cloak' and leads*

135

him to the sleeping place. Then SILENUS *gives the cloak to the* PALE BOY *and climbs the stairs to the tragic stage.*)

μη μεταναστης . . . WOE! WOE! WOE!

Not bad for a satyr for his first go.

(*A burst of Apollo music from the RFH wipes the pleasure off the face of* SILENUS *and he stares up the centre gangway as if he sees* APOLLO *and the flayers coming down it.*
His mouth opens in a silent scream.
Blackout.)